FRED & ETHEL
NOYES
❊ OF ❊
SMITHVILLE
NEW JERSEY

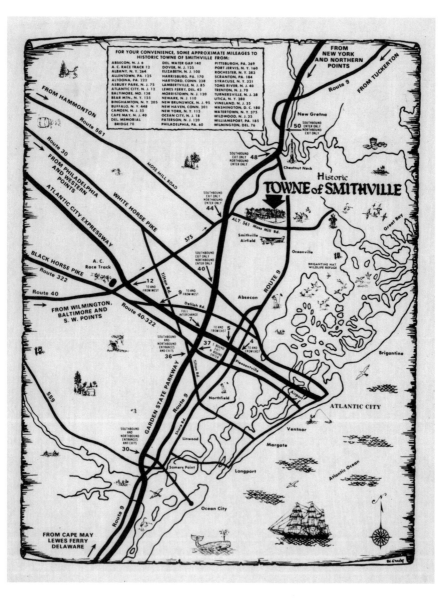

All Roads Lead to the Historic Towne of Smithville, a map. Courtesy of the *Laureate Press*.

FRED & ETHEL
NOYES
❊ OF ❊
SMITHVILLE
NEW JERSEY

THE ARTIST AND THE ENTREPRENEUR

JUDY COURTER

[signature: Judy Courter]

Charleston London

THE
History
PRESS

Published by The History Press
Charleston, SC 29403
www.historypress.net

First published 2013

Manufactured in the United States

ISBN 978.1.62619.032.0

Library of Congress CIP data applied for.

DEDICATION

*To the people who so generously shared with me their memories
and stories about Fred and Ethel.*

*Sid Ascher, Howard Berger, Al (Richard) Black, Roland Bonner, Bob Bowen,
Charles Braun, Francis X. Burke, David Bruce Burrows, Dick Butler, Steve
Calvi, Mae Carrow, Horace Cavileer, John Cavileer, Marge Downs Cavileer, Jack
and Margo Clayton, Kirk Conover, Marge Conover, Tess Conover, Paul Cope,
Sandy Costa, John Cunningham, Ed Davis, George Dehner, John Dermanoski,
Anne (Butera) Fabbri, John Fallucca, Carl Fiore, Margie Cavileer Fox, William
Gemmel, Gary Giberson, Niki Giberson, Jack (and Lucy) Gruhle, Dottie Hammill,
Clarence and Joan Hanselman, Irene Hartman, Ginny Haslam, Harvey Haslett,
Milton (John) and Sophie Heinzer, James Hitchner, Ed Hitzel, Wilbur Hoch,
Lee and Marge Howlett, Michael Hyett, Paul James, Margaret Johnson, Nelson
Johnson, Joseph Kaufmann, Martha Keates, Paxson Keates, Glenn Kennedy, Jane
Betts Kubernus, Bob Kusnirik, Jack and Virginia Lamping, Bertha Lingelbach,
Dave Lingelbach, Betty Loveland, Richard R. Lovett III, Maria at JoJo's
Galloway, Edna Marshall, Jane Marshall, Cindy Mason-Purdie, Dr. James
Mason IV (Cindy's father), Barbara McLaughlin, William and Betty McMahon,
Bess Miller, Florence Miller, Lois Muller, George Nestor, Sophie Nestor, Andy
Newman, Jim Paxson, Don Phillips, David Rhodes, Nancy Rhodes, John Rogge,
Anthony Rudisill, John Scalia, Joyce Schiereck, Antoinette (Toni) Olivier Smith,
Paul Stankard, Barry and Gay Taylor, Helene Walls, Martin Wenig, Catherine
White and Gene Zarillo.*

CONTENTS

CONTENTS

AUTHOR'S NOTE

I began interviewing in 1998. I was racing against time in my efforts to get the story down from those who had lived it. As each individual I spoke with referred me to someone else, my resource network grew, and in 2005, I stopped interviewing and began to write.

All the interviews were vital in producing this chronicle. Although I could not include every anecdote, each was significant in helping me understand how Ethel and Fred accomplished what they did. This dynamic couple came alive for me in the words of those I talked to. The stories made this experience informative and fun.

ACKNOWLEDGEMENTS

I could not have written this book without the help of many people along the way.

For confidence and inspiration, I am grateful to Marge Conover, John Cavileer, Martha Keates, Nelson Johnson, author John Cunningham and my father, Lawrence P. Mills.

I am deeply grateful to my daughter Amanda Courter for the many demanding hours she spent transcribing the taped interviews that are the foundation for this book. Amanda's support and editing entries were invaluable. Thank you also to Courtney Plotts for transcribing.

I thank Alice Chambers, Dave Murphy and Carol Plum-Ucci for reading and critiquing my manuscript. Whitney Tarella Landis at The History Press provided detailed suggestions that greatly improved the book. Emily d'Aulaire, friend and professional writer, steered me through editing the first critical chapters.

Many thanks to Antonietta Vaccarella at ARC Reprographics for diligently scanning and numbering the images for this book.

This work would not have found its way to completion without the talent and support of two special women, Sandy Warren and Tula Christopoulos. I thank Sandy, consultant, writer and promoter, for guidance through the long writing process, and Tula for her dedication and technical expertise.

INTRODUCTION

I will never underestimate the power of a photograph. I had just resigned from an all-consuming job and asked my husband, Joe, to meet me for a drink at the Lantern Light Inn in Smithville. Without knowing it, I was already looking for my next challenge.

Before leaving the tavern that bitter cold night, I went to the ladies' room. I was struck by several photographs hanging on the wall. In one, Ethel Noyes looked out at me from behind black-rimmed glasses. She stood at the edge of Lake Meone in the Historic Towne of Smithville. Next to her was husband, Fred. In a nearby photo, she posed with Fred and Elwood Kirkman, a notorious local lawyer, banker and real estate maverick. The third picture showed Ethel Noyes sitting erect at her antique writing desk. Ethel: founder of Smithville, entrepreneur, a woman ahead of her time.

Why, I wondered, had I never noticed the photos before? I felt suddenly inspired and hurried back to Joe. One by one, we examined the other photographs of Fred and Ethel that filled the tavern walls. Did people who saw these photographs even know who Fred and Ethel Noyes were? Did they know that they were the creators of not only Smithville but also the Ram's Head Inn and the Noyes Museum of Art?

Joe and I knew that Fred and Ethel were interesting personalities who had made significant contributions to South Jersey. We knew their story should not be lost. Yet the only published works we were aware of that devoted a few pages to them were William McMahon's slender volumes about the Historic Inn and Old Village. Ethel had died in 1979; Fred in

1987. Before long, their lives would be forgotten. I determined that day not to let that happen.

Over the next few days, I talked with several people who had known and worked with the Noyeses. Everyone was enthusiastic and encouraged me to write the story. First, I went to the archives of the local newspaper, the *Press of Atlantic City*, to research everything I could find about Fred and Ethel and Smithville. Then I bought a small tape recorder for interviews. My adventure had begun.

Early on, I made a find at an antiques shop in an old chicken coop on the corner of Jim Leeds and Pitney Road in Galloway Township. The owner of the Chicken Coop, Ken Smith, had dealt with the Noyeses often when they hunted for antiques. Fred used to stop by to shoot the breeze, and Ken thought he had some letters of Fred's. The letters turned out to be written in 1933 by Fred's father to a niece when the Noyes family lived in Lower Bank, New Jersey. The Chicken Coop was torn down a few years after my visit to make way for a CVS drugstore, and Ken Smith died a short time later. The living history was fast disappearing.

Ken is one of many people who were delighted to share stories about Fred and Ethel with me. I feel fortunate to have had this chance to relive and record a bit of the past.

I had not written a book before, so I struggled with the task. A number of times, I let the project idle. Sometimes I just plain ran lickety-split in other directions. But Fred and Ethel never let go of me. I came to love and admire this extraordinary man and woman during the fourteen years I worked to record their story. I feel as strongly about Fred and Ethel Noyes today as I did when their photographs spoke to me from the walls of the Lantern Light Inn tavern in Smithville. Their story needs to be told.

Chapter 1

THE HEYDAY

"Fred Noyes, Fred Noyes, paging Fred Noyes. Report to the main office immediately." The loudspeakers of the paging system carried the message over several acres of the Historic Towne of Smithville. Fred was stationed on his favorite barstool in the tavern of the Lantern Light Inn, enjoying a scotch and a moment's respite from his wife, Ethel. Shaking his head slowly with an amused smile, he thought, "There she is, after me again."

The year was 1968, and Smithville was approaching its zenith in a booming economy. With the construction of the Garden State Parkway and the Atlantic City Expressway, southern New Jersey was being discovered anew by travelers. Wide beaches, rolling surf, grand Atlantic City hotels, restaurants, entertainment and the beauty of the marshlands and rural countryside beckoned.

Just fifteen years earlier, Fred had tended bar himself at a makeshift card table set up in the old Smithville Inn. If he didn't know how to make the drink a customer asked for, he had the customer teach him and gave the drink away for free. Now Fred could sit on the other side of the bar at lunchtime, or anytime, as long as he stayed out of Ethel's way. If she found him, she would take away his drink and put him to work.

The bartenders at Smithville were in a tricky position because they had two bosses. Fred and Ethel were the "Possessors" of the Historic Smithville Inns, Inc., a multimillion-dollar business consisting of nine restaurants, fourteen shops, an airstrip, a motel and an outdoor theater. Ethel was a visionary and entrepreneur. She masterminded the daily routine. Fred, an artist, was her mainstay. He defined their business philosophy and had the final say on all major decisions.

Concerned for her portly, diabetic husband's health, Ethel told the bartenders, "If you give Fred a drink, you'll be fired." Fred, the bartenders' other boss, said, "If you *don't* give me a drink, you'll be fired."

That day Fred's ally was Glenn Kennedy, maitre d' at the Lantern Light Inn, a colonial-style restaurant that opened in 1964.

Getting off his barstool, Fred called out, "Glenn, let's have a meeting at the table here in the corner." Fred sat down and put his drink on the floor by his chair to hide it from Ethel's view. Glenn, tall and handsome in formal attire, joined him. The two men were leaning over a notepad of Ethel's instructions for the day when she strode briskly through the door.

Ethel was of average height but appeared taller. Her bearing was exquisitely erect, and she wore her hair pulled up in an immaculate chignon that added to her stature. To maintain this trademark coiffure, Fred drove her to the hairdresser in Philadelphia every week. She wore a belted, high-necked dress tailored perfectly to her trim figure. Cat-eyed, dark-rimmed glasses were prominent on her even-featured face. Only when she smiled did the gap between her teeth hint that there was more to Ethel than studied perfection.

She greeted the patrons in the tavern and nodded curtly at the bartender. After circling the table, Ethel sat down between Fred and Glenn. She crossed her legs and deftly knocked over Fred's drink with the toe of her shoe. With a knowing smile, Ethel said, "Fred, I'm *so* glad I found you. We need to be at the Inn in five minutes for the meeting."

Fred was expected to chair the lunch meeting. It was just that the days were so jam-packed with meetings and chores that he never had a moment to himself. "I did everything Ethel wanted this morning," Fred thought. "This afternoon I'll do a few things of my own and get away from the damn paging system."

It had been a busy morning for Fred and Ethel. The couple had been up since dawn to drive from their home in nearby Port Republic to oversee morning deliveries to the restaurants. There was excitement in the air. The grounds crew was on the job early to get ready for the crowds that would come on Sunday from as far as New York and Philadelphia for the renowned Mother's Day buffet. The grass was getting a final trim, and the damp earth around the daffodils and tulips was raked to perfection. Inside, decisions were made for flowers to decorate the dining tables and the buffet. Ethel's brother-in-law, Bob Muller, was completing calculations for the food order based on past statistics and the weather forecast.

It took many unglamorous hours behind the scenes for the glamorous event to happen. Ethel had been up during the night completing lists of tasks to be done on a pad she kept by her bedside. In addition to staffing, food and flowers, all fourteen shops needed to be checked. There was extra inventory to be unpacked and displayed to entice Sunday's visitors. This was delegated to Fred, a job that suited him because he liked to be outside and to shoot the breeze with the shop managers.

Ethel expected her employees to work hard, but no one worked harder than she did. It was a joke among the restaurant staff that, although the menu items had not changed, the menus were physically larger so that Ethel could write more notes and instructions on the back. Her aspirations knew no bounds. Currently, she was creating an Old Village in the style of Williamsburg or Sturbridge to replicate life in South Jersey in the year 1815.

After the lunch meeting that day, Ethel went to supervise the reconstruction of the gristmill that had been dismantled and moved piece by piece from Sharptown, New Jersey. Fred went to his office, where he kept his paints and an easel. He was an artist and painted every chance he got. He was working on a still life of brilliant primary colors, but when he looked at his watch and saw it was 4:00 p.m., he knew it was time to take the only break he and Ethel would get in their long day. Reluctantly, he wiped his paintbrushes clean. Ethel took good care of Fred, but she forgot to take care of herself—she had a weak heart. So Fred insisted they take a break every day. If it were up to Ethel, they would go to the grocery store to look for special seasonal items or run some other errand. Fred liked to go home for a short rest before driving back to supervise the dinner hour.

Smithville took on a new pulse after five. The Smithville Inn came alive with a vast wood-burning fireplace, candlelight, fresh linen, the smell of baking chicken potpies and the bustle of waitresses dressed in colonial costume. Ethel was everywhere, spot-checking the dinner plates as they came out of the kitchen, managing the hostess podium in the lobby and working the dining room, speaking to all the guests. Fred stationed himself, drink nearby, on a stool at the entrance to the Great Bay room to chat and joke with customers.

When Ethel overheard two new waitresses make a plan to meet other employees after the restaurant closed, she admonished, "None of that, young ladies, it's home and to bed for you. Tomorrow is one of our busiest days, and you'll need every ounce of energy you can muster from a good night's sleep." Ethel knew all too well that many of the staff enjoyed time together after a hard night's work. One group went to Jo Jo's Bar, a couple miles south on New York Road, and another on to the Beachcomber Bar and Restaurant. Ethel worried that an errant employee might drink too much and get into an automobile accident. These thoughts in mind, she added abruptly before she left the room, "I don't want you girls ending up in a ditch somewhere." The waitresses cast a glance at each other. They didn't quite know what to think of Ethel. She was very strict, but she cared about them and treated them like family.

Before leaving for the night, Fred and Ethel had one more job to do. They walked around to all fourteen stores in the Shoppes at Smithville to be sure the window displays were perfect for the next day. A note was left for the shopkeeper if anything was awry. On the way home, Fred drove quietly while Ethel's mind whirled busily with thoughts of new waitresses, building renovations and tomorrow's buffet. She would ask Fred to help her decide which of her three new outfits she should wear. Then she leaned back and forced herself to relax for a moment.

Suddenly, she sat up with a start and exclaimed, "Oh, Fred, I don't see how we can make it through the year without more financing. The Old Village restoration is costing thousands and makes no money. Our finances are stretched to the limit."

Fred was well aware of the precarious financial situation. But it was his role to relieve the tension. "We will find a way, Ethel," he replied. "We always have."

Chapter 2

A PORTRAIT OF THE ARTIST
AS A YOUNG MAN

O n April 19, 1905, horses and carriages could be heard making their way through the rain and mud on Philadelphia's Broad Street. Inside, at 1210 South Broad, no heed was paid to it. Louisa Bond Noyes had been in labor with her third child through a long, restless night. Early that morning, she asked her husband, Fred, to go for the doctor. Her dark, wavy hair was damp with perspiration and clung in startling contrast to the white skin of her face and neck. She had a prominent, patrician nose and dark brown, deep-set eyes. The firm line of her mouth displayed strength and stubborn determination. The doctor arrived, and after several more hours of struggle, a bawling baby boy was delivered.

Fred Winslow Noyes Jr. was born into a loving family and a world of material comfort. His father held a high position in the textile industry, and his mother was part of the wealthy and socially prominent Bond family. Fred Sr. had studied at the Lowell School of Design in Boston and worked in the Sanford Mills in Maine. His love of textile design drew him to Philadelphia, which was the hub of the industrial revolution in the late 1800s. From 1886 to 1906, Fred was one of the highest-paid men in Philadelphia's thriving textile business.

Along with a highly successful career came an entrée into Philadelphia society and an invitation to the Bond home. There Fred met and gained the adoration of Louisa K. Bond, daughter of Mary Geese Bond and adopted daughter of James. A careless nursemaid had dropped Louisa when she was an infant, and her left hand had been broken. Her hand did not heal properly and became withered. But Louisa never let this deter her from carrying herself as proudly as the other girls of Philadelphia society.

The stately Bond residence on Broad Street was richly decorated with heavy brocade drapes, ornate carved Victorian sofas, Oriental carpets and fine oil portraits. Burgundy flocked wallpaper and a long oak dining table with high-backed chairs and partner sideboards with silver tea service set the tone for formal family dinners. Christmas was lavish. The first floor was decorated with holly and pine boughs, and mistletoe hung in the doorways. Elaborate menus were printed for the sumptuous meal. Fred Noyes Sr.'s presence at the 1894 Christmas dinner was duly noted by his signature on the menu.

Fred Noyes and Louisa Bond were married in 1895. Two daughters, Mary and Evelyn, were born in the next three years. The girls were nine and seven by the time Fred—or Fritz, as he came to be called—was born. Fritz was the baby of the family. His two older sisters doted on him, and as the only son, he maintained a favored place in his parents' eyes. Early on, Fritz showed an interest in art, and he was allowed to play with the little box of cards that held his father's colorful paisley textile designs.

The good life was shattered by tragedy when Fritz was thirteen years old. The flu pandemic of 1918 killed twenty-five to forty million people worldwide and more than five hundred thousand Americans. Philadelphia was hit with a vengeance. Oddly, young adults were most vulnerable. In October, the flu claimed the lives of Mary Noyes, twenty-two years old, and three of Louisa's half sisters. The Noyeses' other daughter, Evelyn, was weakened by the illness and died two years later. They were all buried in the Woodlands Cemetery in Philadelphia. Fritz escaped the ravages of the flu, but lost two loving sisters. He became even more treasured by his parents and bonded closely with them.

Louisa relied on the toughness and resiliency she inherited from her mother to deal with so many family deaths. Mary Geese Bond had buried two husbands and five of her eight children, and she never admitted to being over fifty-five years old. Mary's great-grandson Richard Lovett III remarked, "All the women in the family were very well preserved. They aged very well, and they all lied about their age."

Louisa also maintained strength through nourishing family relationships. Her only remaining half sister, Edith, and her husband, Richard Lovett Sr., bought a house in Longport, New Jersey in 1921. Longport is a quiet seashore town on the southern tip of Absecon Island. At the north end of this nine-mile-long barrier island off the New Jersey coast was Atlantic

City, rowdy and awake all night with its gambling parlors, drinking saloons and brothels.

Louisa, Fred Sr. and Fritz visited the Lovetts at the Jersey Shore in the summer. Cool ocean breezes and the lulling sound of surf provided a pleasant gathering place for the extended Bond family away from the heat and frenzy of Philadelphia. A photograph from that time showed Fritz standing on the beach between his parents, all looking like they were ready to walk down Broad Street rather than stroll in the sand.

The long, lazy days in Longport were spent with the Lovett cousins and grandparents Mary Geese and James Bond. Fritz was the eldest of the cousins and the leader of summer fun and mischief. A good-looking boy, he was interested in girls early on. He flirted with and teased the daughters of neighboring families, including Fernanda Wanamaker.

Fritz also found time to paint. He painted his grandfather, James Bond, seated on the porch in a slat-backed rocking chair. This portrait hangs on the wall of the Lovett family home in Longport today.

Back in Philadelphia, the Noyeses lived at 4811 Leiper Street in the Frankford section. Fritz attended Frankford High School, where he took a mechanical arts course and his first formal art training. He was now called Fred, except among family and close friends. Fred left high school at the start of his senior year in October 1922. It is not known what he did the next four years other than paint. In 1926, he began taking art courses at night at the Philadelphia Industrial Art School (now the Philadelphia College of Art) at Broad and Pine Streets. He studied antiques, a subject of great value to him later, and still-life painting. Fred applied himself wholeheartedly to his studies and convinced his father and grandfather that his intentions were serious and not "young trifling ideas."

In September 1928, he applied to the Pennsylvania Academy of the Fine Arts, writing, "Portrait painting and illustrating are the two ambitions of my life in art. So after consideration of my love for art and nothing else in particular, my father has consented to send me to your day classes." Fred was accepted by the academy and took an apartment on Penn Street. He studied composition, construction, life, still life and perspective. According to school records, he was a dedicated student.

As the stock market steadily ascended, opportunities for riches and success seemed boundless. Just one month before Fred entered the academy, President Herbert Hoover proclaimed, "We in America today are nearer to the final triumph over poverty than ever before in the history of any land." Then on October 29, 1929, the stock market crashed and the nation plunged into the deepest and most prolonged economic depression in its history. Severe unemployment took hold, ranging from 25 to 80 percent. Cities in the industrial northeast were paralyzed, especially in areas where textile mills and coal mines were closed. The Great Depression became a depression of the American spirit as well as the economy.

The fortunes of the Noyes family changed with the times. Fred applied for free tuition for his fourth year of study at the academy. His letter to the Committee on Instruction stated that he had no money but would live with his parents and earn enough for supplies. "This year I cannot receive the help of my parents that I generally get," and in parentheses, he wrote "due to my father's illness." Like others, the Depression assaulted Fred Noyes Sr.'s health as well as his finances.

Fred was accepted as a scholarship student, and consequently, his work had to be reviewed every month. The approach of the academy was classical, based in art history. If a student's work was not considered acceptable by these standards, he was told to change his style. Fred and several of his colleagues frequented Philadelphia galleries, such as the Newman Galleries on Walnut Street. There they admired the work of the abstract movement popular in Europe at the time. The young artists were inspired by Paul Cézanne's analytical flat planes and the bright primitive colors and energetic brush strokes of Andre Derain and Henri Matisse. Fred experimented boldly with the new style. This was not acceptable to the academy, and he was told to leave.

The Great Depression rose to full force and continued to send shock waves throughout the country. Fred Sr. was close to losing his job, and his health was fragile. "All his friends in the textile industry had killed themselves because of bad times. The doctor told my father to get the hell out of town before he killed himself," Fred recalled later. Fred Sr. loved to fish, so when he found a summer cottage for sale on the Mullica River in South Jersey, he bought it for $1,000.

The place did not have heat or running water. There was no insulation, and when it got cold in the winter, Fred Sr. had to put coverings on the walls. In the summer, the bungalow was covered with climbing roses. The cottage was in the town of Lower Bank on the north shore of the Mullica River, midway between the historic iron furnaces of Batsto to the west and the mouth of the river at Chestnut Neck to the east.

Lower Bank was on the edge of the Pine Barrens, a forested area almost as large as Yosemite Park. The Pine Barrens are flat, and the land is sandy, covered with dwarf forest, mostly pine and some oak. Under the sand is an extensive aquifer of pure, soft water, a precious resource for a populous state. Starting in colonial times when smugglers sought hiding places, many colorful characters have inhabited the Pine Barrens. The legend of the Jersey Devil, born of Mother Leeds in the 1700s, took place there. During the American Revolution and War of 1812, bog iron was mined from the bogs, streams and waterways. Towns grew around the furnaces where the material was forged into cannon balls, weapons and camp tools. With the demise of the iron industry in the mid-1800s, only ghost towns and the fiercely independent remained. These self-sufficient individuals were called "Pineys." They treasured their isolation and ability to live off the land.

"There's a smell of the Mullica that ain't like any other smell on earth. Once you get the smell of the Mullica up your nose, all other smells are stinks," said Piney Charlie Leek.

Fred was twenty-seven years old when he moved with his parents to Lower Bank. The secluded rural life had an indelible impact on him, his painting and, later, his interest in carving and decoy collecting. This main line Philadelphia family might have expected difficulty adjusting to the remote and unsophisticated Pine Barrens. On the contrary, they seemed to thrive.

Fred's mother, the bird-like Louisa, was an exacting housewife who liked to keep everything shipshape, so the rigors of rustic living on the Mullica were a challenge. "Don't look like the country club set, do we? Well, that's what we were! Always going to something, always entertaining or being entertained. If anybody had told me then that we'd come down to a place like Lower Bank and love every minute of it, I'd have told them they were being very silly. Now—well, we just couldn't go back to that other life again."

The garrulous Fred Sr. integrated easily into the casual Piney society. He became the self-proclaimed Mayor of Lower Bank. No longer needing to be a natty dresser, the Mayor developed a passion for old clothes and didn't bother to shave every day. He befriended many of the locals and pursued the history of Lower Bank families, including the Leeks, the Sooys and the Cavileers. On his neighborly ramblings, he would often bring home tomato plants, artichokes and Chinese cabbage plants to turn over to Fritz, who helped tend the garden.

A keen observer of the flora and fauna in the pines, the Mayor was sensitive to the spiritual power of nature. He wrote a series of letters to his niece Nodi in 1933, titled "Bungalow Life in the Jersey Pines." The letters were typed on paper of varying degrees of yellow and brown. Pen and ink drawings of flowers and ferns meticulously colored and shaded with colored pencil adorned the pages. There were sketches of tiny deer heads and footprints, yellow and black box turtles, pine snakes and laundry blowing in the breeze. Paisley design drawings also appeared in these letters, a theme later seen in Fred Jr.'s art.

Commenting later on the move to Lower Bank, the Mayor said, "A year they gave me…that was over ten years ago, and I'm better now than I ever was."

Following his parents "take it as it comes and enjoy it" attitude, Fred Jr. quickly adapted to the bucolic life along the Mullica and thrived. They gardened, trapped and fished, and when it got cold in the pines, they just put more wood on the fire.

Meanwhile, history-making events were taking place in the Philadelphia art world. Albert Barnes, a modern art advocate, was negotiating to donate his extensive collection of contemporary European art to the Pennsylvania Academy of the Fine Arts. The academy, however, judged his collection to be unorthodox and refused it. Mr. Barnes, whose collection is now known as one of the finest in the world, was upset. When he heard about the coterie of students following the modern style who had been thrown out of the academy, Barnes invited them to study with him in Merion, Pennsylvania. Fred and several others accepted. They lived and studied with Barnes at no charge for two years, from 1936 to 1938. Barnes had a reputation for being difficult. When asked later what he thought of Barnes, Fred said Barnes was a wonderful man. The only time Barnes ever got angry was if a student walked in on him while he was with one of the models.

On March 17, 1937, there was an introductory exhibition of Fred's paintings at the Boyer Galleries in Philadelphia. The works *Rube's House* and *My Stove* were subjects straight from the Jersey Pines. One reviewer found some of the still lifes "little more than imitation. But when one turns to such pictures as *The Last Haul*, *Passing the Seine* and *Frozen River*, with its blood red sun, one finds a decidedly personal inflection in Mr. Noyes's work, and style, which he would do well to develop. A growth in effort to plumb the inner sense of things is apparent in the paintings by Fred Noyes."

Another exhibition of Fred's drawings in color and black and white at the Warwick Galleries drew further comment: "The liberals in art will find much to delight eye and mind in the exhibition. There is a suggestion of Klee and Kandinsky in many of the designs. One senses the artist's ability as a possible designer for pottery or textiles."

On returning home to Lower Bank at the age of thirty-three, Fred continued to devote himself to painting. He drew and painted what was around him: men fishing with nets, sunsets, trees and a Piney cottage. Fred invited neighbor Horace Cavileer, then a high school student, to sit for a portrait. Fred often wore his French artist's beret and seemed like a person who didn't have a care in the world. His neighbor Marge Cavileer thought he was "a lazy kind of fella." Horace Cavileer agreed: "None of them [the Noyes family] worked, not even Fred. He used to draw pictures, paint pictures and all that stuff." Painting with the goal of creating art was not considered work on the Mullica. Fred, however, didn't worry about what anyone thought.

Fred had a good time hobnobbing with the families in the area. He was close with Walter K. Cavileer Jr., a fishing buddy who lived a few houses west of the Noyes cottage on River Road. Walter dated Marge Downs from nearby Wading River, and Marge remembered Fred's love interests. One was Madeline Vautrinot, a slender, good-looking young woman with dark hair from Egg Harbor City. Madeline was also an artist. Fred knew his mother liked Madeline and wanted him to marry her. But Fred did not follow his mother's advice, and Madeline married Sonny Fraser from the Fraser family of the Atlantic City Country Club and Atlantic City Racetrack.

Life on the Mullica was about to end for Fred. When the Germans invaded Poland in September 1939 and Britain and France declared war on Germany, the United States isolationist policy changed. The country shifted to a stance of preparedness and began to expand its armed forces, build defense plants and supply war materials to the Allies. Fred Jr. would be among the first to be recruited under the Selective Training and Service Act that became law on September 16, 1940.

When he left Lower Bank, he took with him a love of nature and a simple way of life. So strong was the influence of the Jersey Pines that later many people thought of him as a Piney, for he had tucked away his urban roots. Fritz's later paintings continued to draw from his experiences on the Mullica, full of fish, rivers and skies bright with sunlit colors.

Chapter 3

THE BEGINNINGS OF A WOMAN
AHEAD OF HER TIME

E thel Marie Lingelbach was born into a vastly different world from Fred
Winslow Noyes Jr., even though it was less than sixty miles away. In the
parlors on Broad Street, Ethel's Native American heritage would have been
a source of gossip and speculation. But in South Jersey, Ethel never had to
hide it. In fact, she was proud that her paternal great-great-grandmother
was a full-blooded member of the Leni-Lenape tribe that lived near the
Mullica River.

Ethel's Native American heritage came through her father, Chris Doughty
Lingelbach. The Lingelbachs had come to the United States in the 1850s
from Lingelbach, Germany, a town near Munich. Chris's father, Franz,
settled on Wrangleboro Road in Hewittown, one of South Jersey's forgotten
towns, near present-day Port Republic. There Franz met and married Anna
Hewitt, whose grandmother was Leni-Lenape.

Ethel's grandparents on her mother's side had also emigrated from
Germany. Oswald and Marie Priebs and their two children came from
Dresden in the late 1800s. They brought only a couple boxes, some fine
linen and a big coffeepot that Marie used for cooking as well as making
coffee. They settled in Philadelphia on the Delaware River waterfront and
had two more children. When Oswald saw land advertised for sale by a
German stock company, he took the train to South Jersey and bought twenty
acres in Pomona. The family moved there, cleared the land by hand and
built a house. Oswald Priebs never stopped working. When the sun went
down, he'd grab a lantern and continue grubbing out tree stumps or turning

over soil. The Priebs had three more children. Marie worked as hard as her husband to provide a comfortable and secure home for their seven children, of whom Caroline was the fourth.

While the Priebs were laboring in Pomona, the Lingelbachs were also farming and raising a family five miles away in Hewittown. Franz and Anna Hewitt had six children. Chris Doughty Lingelbach was their second child and eldest son, born in March 1886.

When he was in his early twenties, Chris's job was to drive the horse-drawn mail wagon from town to town. He was on his way to the train station in Pomona on a crisp autumn day in 1908 when the piercing whistle of an approaching train startled the horse and he reared. Chris stood and shouted and pulled hard on the reins of the frightened animal. This only made matters worse, and when the horse whinnied and reared again, Chris lost his balance and fell backward into his wagon. A female's high-spirited laugh rang in the air. Chris looked in the direction of the humiliating sound and saw a slim girl with wavy chestnut hair and a wide grin looking straight at him. The horse, quiet now that the train whistle had subsided, stood stock-still and innocent while Chris righted himself and jumped down from the wagon. The girl had separated herself from the others on the train platform, who were no longer interested now that the entertainment was over. Caroline Priebs, however, kept her attention on the agile, fresh-faced youth who approached her. Chris good-naturedly challenged Caroline to drive the wagon. As she took up the reins, a romance and lifelong union began.

It did not take Chris and Caroline long to realize they came from similar backgrounds and shared common values and goals. They married in 1910 and settled on a corner of Chris's family farm on Wrangleboro Road. Then Caroline's father, Oswald, became ill, his constitution broken by years of hard physical labor on the farm. Even the healing touch of his wife, Marie, could not save him. Oswald died in midwinter, shortly before his first grandchild was born.

Caroline Priebs Lingelbach went to her mother's house in Pomona when it was time for her baby to be born. There, she gave birth to a daughter, Ethel Marie, on March 8, 1911. Ethel was given the middle name Marie in honor of her grandmother.

Ethel Marie didn't lack attention from her mother and grandmothers, but it was her father who became the star of her universe. Kind, intelligent and humorous, Chris Lingelbach doted on his first child. He took her with him whenever he could. He regaled the toddler with stories about the neighbors, countryside and folklore of the area.

When Caroline became pregnant with their second child, the young couple decided to find a house in town near a school and other families. Ethel was a year and a half old when her father took her house hunting.

The Lingelbachs found a two-bedroom bungalow in Pleasantville on Oneida Street. Chris cleared the lot on one side of the house to farm. In the back was a barn for a milking cow. Everett was born in the large first-floor bedroom on May 6, 1913. Grandmother Priebs was again on hand to help. Ethel was a pensive three-year-old in a ruffled white dress when she was photographed standing by a chair where baby Ev, also in a white dress, was propped. Two and a half years later, Caroline gave birth to another girl named Bertha. When Bertha was old enough, she joined Ethel and Ev in the bedroom they shared.

While Caroline tended her rapidly growing family, Chris gardened and sold milk. The United States entered World War I in 1917, and Chris joined the National Guard in Mays Landing, the county seat. The extra income helped support a growing family, for Caroline was pregnant again with their fourth child. Harry was born on a winter day in February 1919. Grandma Priebs had help this time. Bertha, who was three and a half years old, said, "I remember Doc Alan came with his little black satchel. I thought he brought my baby brother Hap in that bag."

The Lingelbach children walked to the Woodland Avenue School on Main Street. One of Ethel's classmates described her as prissy but well liked. She planned the games for schoolmates and told everyone what to do. Although she was bossy, she was popular and a leader.

By 1922, the family of six was outgrowing the Pleasantville house and Chris wanted more land to farm. Ethel was eleven years old when the family moved a few miles north to a farmhouse in Oceanville. Oceanville is on Old New York Road, now known as Route 9, a road that stretches along the New Jersey coast from New York City south to Atlantic City and then on to the tip of the state in Cape May. Now part of Galloway Township, Oceanville is easy to miss as one travels on Old New York Road today. But in the 1920s, it was a hub of activity with the Brigantine spur of the Atlantic City Railroad running right through town.

The Lingelbach home was classic "Jersey Shore" Victorian. There was a parlor, dining room, kitchen and pantry on the first floor, three bedrooms and a bathroom on the second floor and an attic on the third floor. Lois was born in the new house in July 1925. Ethel was fourteen years old.

Chris now had a regular farm, not just a city lot, and he expanded the marketing of his produce. He began huckstering in Atlantic City, taking his produce and selling it at the municipal market or bartering for other things the family needed. Bertha and Hap liked to go with their father, but Ethel never did. She wasn't an outdoor person. She liked to read and would often go into the attic with a book to get away from everyone. One of Chris's customers gave him a set of Elsie Dinsmore books that became Ethel's favorite reading. Elsie was inquisitive and lively, and she lived in a fantasy world of gilt carriages, prison ships, beggars and kings.

One sweltering summer day when Ethel was sixteen, her mother, Caroline, gathered the girls to go blackberry picking at Grandma Priebs's. They wore jumpsuits to keep from getting scratched by the thorns and straw hats to protect them from the burning sun. With tin berry buckets in tow, they got in the big black Ford and drove to Pomona.

When they got to the berry patch, Ethel was last out of the back of the car, where her book was tucked in a corner. Caroline was eager to get them started picking. After picking a handful of berries, Ethel brushed away a whining mosquito, tossed her head defiantly and said, "The heck with this!" Without a backward glance toward her mother or sisters, she got in the car and nestled in the back corner with an Elsie Dinsmore book.

The Lingelbachs' social life revolved around family. As Bertha explained it, "There was no one else; everything was really just family. We were called the foreigners; Germans you know." Ethel was always trying to get her Grandma Priebs to talk about life in Dresden before she and Oswald came to this country. Grandma Priebs told of a carriage lined in velvet that came to pick her up and take her to a portrait artist. The portrait hung in a museum in Dresden.

Although Grandpa Oswald was gone, the Priebs farm remained a place of hard work and simple pleasures. Every Saturday, the girls scrubbed the wooden farmhouse floors. In the fall, there was a pig slaughter, and all the family came to help. Grandmother Priebs labored over the wood stove making sausage, liverwurst and scrapple. She cooked the heart of the pig and gave the children slices on homemade bread. Grandmudder, as she was called, had no recipe book.

One night, for no reason at all, Ethel wanted a clown suit. Whenever Ethel wanted something, Ethel got it. Grandmudder went through all her rags and scraps of cloth; they saved everything in those days. She had a treadle sewing machine, and before the Lingelbachs went home, Ethel had her clown suit.

All the aunts, uncles and cousins gathered on Sunday at Granmudder Priebs's home and spent the day cooking, talking, playing games and eating. After dinner, the adults played pinochle around a huge table while the children roamed the farm and the outbuildings. The extended family got to know each other well, and cousins were as close as brothers and sisters.

One relative Ethel spent a lot of time with was Aunt Daisy Conover, Chris Lingelbach's youngest sister. Like Chris, she was interested in the history and folklore of the region. Daisy and Ethel drove around the countryside to look for old houses and bargain for antiques at yard sales. Inspired by Aunt Daisy, Ethel read everything she could about South Jersey's past. She asked questions about antiques to learn what was valuable and what wasn't. She began to collect things, including a cobbler's bench and a spinning wheel.

Ethel set an example for her younger brothers and sisters as a good student at the one-room Oceanville schoolhouse that served as the classroom for thirty students up to eighth grade. Her father and her uncle had only gone to school through the third grade. In her eighth-grade graduation photograph taken in 1924, Ethel looked petulant and plump. She was thirteen and weighed nearly 160 pounds. She didn't want anyone to see the photograph and became determined to solve her weight problem. She was never overweight again, and being slender became an important part of her image. She was known to eat bird-like half portions, leading some people to think she was anorexic. Even in her sixties, a reporter described her as "willow-like."

Ethel took the commercial course of study at Atlantic City High School. She studied typing, commercial arithmetic, stenography and office practices. Most of the Lingelbachs took this track instead of college preparation. Far from exceptional, Ethel's graduation average was seventy-three. She was regarded as take-charge and fun-loving and had many friends. She graduated in 1928 with no apparent dream or concept of what she wanted to do. Her first job was at Wilson's Dairy on New York Avenue in Atlantic City. The dairy luncheonette, well known for its delicious sandwiches displayed in a glass case, was located across from the Schwinn Building. People came from all around to get their lunches there. Ethel's job was to make sandwiches and to wait on customers at the counter, an experience that would serve her well in her future at Smithville.

After a year, she moved on to work at the Singer Sewing Shop on Atlantic Avenue, where she became manager. She furthered her business experience in bookkeeping and sales and did sewing demonstrations through the 1930s. She was an excellent seamstress and made the bridal gown and bridesmaid dresses for a friend's wedding. The sewing business thrived during these years, as the area felt the effects of hard economic times.

South Jersey did not escape the Great Depression, but it was different from the cities. In rural areas, there was less to lose. People were more self-reliant and used to making do with what they had. They grew their own food. Caroline canned everything from their garden, so no one went hungry in the Lingelbach household. Most women sewed their family's clothes to save money and did not indulge in ready-to-wear clothes. Even runs in silk stockings were mended. Bert Lingelbach used to make all her clothes, but she was very proud of two dresses she bought, two for five dollars.

During this time, Chris Lingelbach began "bobtailing" to supplement the family income. The bobtailer "cut short" the distance between the wholesaler and the customer by buying products in bulk and then selling them door-to-door. Chris bought bread from Freihofer's Bakery and milk from Wilson's Dairy, both in Atlantic City, and then made deliveries in the Oceanville area. The Bakery and Dairy made their deliveries to the Lingelbach farm at 5:00 a.m. Chris loaded up his truck every day except Sunday and left at daylight to take milk and bread to his customers. His bobtailing business grew rapidly, and he soon needed to enlist the help of his family. Bert went with her father on Saturdays when she was still in high school. She even baked cookies to sell. They tried to collect as they went along, but not everybody could pay. There was a book with a page for each customer. If people didn't have the money, Chris would say, "Okay, when you get it." He trusted everybody.

Chris's territory grew so large that he had two routes and recruited Ethel to help Bertha. He used the truck for his longer route and gave his daughters the Model A Ford. Ethel did the driving over the rutted dirt roads, and Bertha was in charge of the order book. There were about forty or fifty customers, and most had a standard order, such as rye bread or sweet raisin buns. Ethel collected the money and made change out of an old cigar box.

The sisters' delivery route took them north from Oceanville to New Gretna and then west to Leektown, across the Wading River to Green Bank on the Mullica River. From there, they headed east along the Mullica to Lower Bank. The first stop on River Road was the Cavileers, a large family of clammers who had a shed behind their house where the clams from the day's harvest were sorted and prepared for market. The girls' favorite stop was the next-to-last house before the bridge. It was a small place overrun with roses and a garden wild with artichokes and Chinese cabbages.

This was the home of "Mayor Noyes." When the Lingelbach sisters made their delivery of fresh bread, the Mayor came out to greet them in his rumpled plaid shirt and tattered hat. He always had something funny to say. The girls had their fun, too, when the Mayor's son Fritz was around, which he usually was. He emerged from the house sleepy-eyed, and his father, who had clearly been up for hours, would ask if he had enjoyed his cold porridge.

Fritz was a dark, slim, good-looking young man at least five years older than Ethel. He wore a black French artist's beret cocked on the side of his head and a little scarf at his throat. Brandishing a slender paintbrush in the air, he bantered with Ethel and Bertha, much in the manner of his father. When the girls completed their delivery, they got in the Model A and were barely a few yards down the road before they burst into giggles. They stopped at Grandmother Priebs's farm in Pomona and regaled her with stories of their adventures.

These were the first few times Ethel Lingelbach and Fritz Noyes met. They didn't show any interest in each other, according to Bertha. None whatsoever.

Chapter 4

THE WAR YEARS

In February 1941, just three months before his thirty-sixth birthday, Fred was drafted into the infantry. Men were called up on the basis of the classification they received from their local draft board. Men classified 1A were available for induction, with the older men being drafted ahead of the younger ones. Fred's idyllic life on the Mullica came to an end when he was sent to Fort Dix for training.

The base was less than an hour's drive north in central New Jersey, but the lifestyle change was drastic. Fred went from unhurried, impromptu days on the Mullica to the structured regime of the military. Walt Cavileer Jr. and his fiancée, Marge Downs, visited Fred at Fort Dix. It was raining so hard that Marge stayed in the car when they got there. The camping grounds where the recruits stayed in tents had turned to mud. Marge observed, "Fred was a person who seemed like he didn't have a care in the world." With a rifle slung over his shoulder, he wore his metal helmet at a jaunty angle and had a big smile on his face. His cocky stance belied a soldier preparing to go to war. Fred joked with friends that he was glad he was in the infantry, not the cavalry. If he were commanded to retreat, he wanted to go fast. He didn't want to have to drag a horse behind him.

In 1942, Ethel was thirty-one years old and ready for a change. She had worked at Singer Sewing Machine in Atlantic City for over a decade while living with her family. During the Depression, young people often lived at home until married and, even then, stayed in one of the family households until they were established and able to live on their own. The average marriage age rose during the 1930s, and the birthrate declined. Ethel had several suitors, recalled her sister Lois. "She was very popular, very active, she was seriously dating. I remember she dated this one fellow from Boston for quite awhile. Very thick Boston accent. There was another fellow from Philadelphia; he was a rower, very active along Boathouse Row."

Neither young man suited Ethel, however. She had her mind set on other things.

The new rationing boards proved a rare opportunity for Ethel Marie Lingelbach. When the Office of Price Administration (OPA) established an office in Egg Harbor City, she applied for a position. The Ration Board served a number of neighboring communities, including Hammonton, Mays Landing and Absecon and recruited workers from the area as temporary wartime civil servants. Ethel was older and had more experience than the other applicants, and she was readily appointed the chief clerk. Jane Betts (the future Mrs. Kubernus), from Absecon, newly graduated from Pleasantville High School and friend of Ethel's youngest sister, Lois; Ruth Oberfeld, from Egg Harbor City; and Merta Adams, from Port Republic, all worked for Ethel until the office closed in 1945. Jane spent a lot of time with the Lingelbach family, as did Ruth, who later married Ev Lingelbach.

The office was located in the Commercial Bank building on Philadelphia Avenue, the wide main street in downtown Egg Harbor City. It was a hub of activity where everyone served by the board had to come in for their monthly ration stamps. The office provided good, friendly service, but everybody followed the rules. If someone ran out of ration coupons before the allotted time, they would just have to get by without sugar or gas until their next coupons were available. Irate customers were turned over to Ethel to placate.

Ethel Lingelbach got to know a lot of people in Atlantic County during that time, and they got to know her. She kept her desktop so highly polished that it captured her reflection. She was a pretty young woman, with dark hair pulled back and wide-set eyes. Her smile was warm and direct and served her well when dealing with testy customers.

Fred Noyes Sr. came to the Egg Harbor City office regularly, and he and Ethel renewed their acquaintance from the bread and milk route days. The Mayor of Lower Bank kept Ethel up to date on Fred Jr.'s experiences on the Western Front and urged her to write to him.

All the Lingelbach family was involved in the war effort. Ev worked in Camden at the shipyard, Bert worked at Freihofer's Bakery and volunteered for the United Service Organization (USO), Hap enlisted in the medical

THE ARTIST AND THE ENTREPRENEUR

corps and Lois worked at the Naval Air Station in Atlantic City (Bader Field) and Egg Harbor Township (Atlantic City Airport).

"Every spare minute, you were doing something for the war effort. You wouldn't think not to be doing something for the war, you just did," said Jane Betts Kubernus.

After training at Fort Dix, Fred was sent to France. His memories of that time were vividly recorded in a 1981 interview with the *Press of Atlantic City* reporter Ed Hitzel. "In France, I walked into a tank. It was buried. We got hit with an 88 and it took out the whole platoon. That's what we were supposed to do, draw fire, and we did. It took out about half of us."

He was stationed in Nancy, near Strasbourg, when his regiment was ordered to attack a German stronghold on a hill. Fritz carried a Browning Automatic Rifle (BAR), a heavy gun built for a strong soldier. The troops hugged the ground as they ascended the crest of the hill. The Germans had a large cannon dug in to shoot from the top of the hill, but it was aimed to shoot over the attackers' heads. As the Allies got closer, the Germans lowered the barrel and shot the shells right down the hill. Fred was out of bullets and stopped to wait for more ammunition. In a split second, one of the German shells shot down the hill, ricocheted off a piece of wood and lodged in his leg. The impact sent him sprawling but earned him a Purple Heart and a trip home—even though it was on a stretcher.

The injury was serious, and there was a chance he wouldn't walk again. He was sent to the best hospital in the country for limb wounds, the Thomas England General Hospital in Atlantic City, located in the Chalfonte–Haddon Hall Hotel, which is now Resorts Casino Hotel. The facility was one of forty-seven hotels commandeered by the military. It was turned into a four-thousand-bed institution and the largest amputee hospital in the world. The basement housed the Artificial Limb Shop, a cluttered place where amputees shopped for prostheses. It was manned by two shifts of thirty-eight soldiers, and they fitted out one hundred amputees a month.

The resort by the sea had become a vast wartime army base. The only town in the United States to be taken over by the government, Atlantic City was known as Camp Boardwalk from 1942 to 1946. The military moved into the oceanfront hotels one by one in what many remember as the city's finest hour. A former resident recalled that he did not think it unusual when he and his family were given twenty-four hours to leave their hotel apartment and move into his grandparents' home.

When Atlantic City residents walked out of their homes, they were on a military installation. There were German U-boats off the shore, and

German agents had been arrested sneaking ashore on nearby Long Beach Island. Consequently, the army imposed dimouts requiring outdoor lighting and headlights be dimmed and blackout curtains used on the windows of beachfront homes and businesses. Military police guarded the train and bus stations, and the Coast Guard sentries patrolled the beach with dogs.

In the span of four years, the city became the temporary home for three hundred thousand soldiers before they went off to war. The soldiers loved Camp Boardwalk. They were not confined to barracks, could parade on the boardwalk and could go to the Steel Pier for entertainment. At the converted Traymore Hotel, their accommodations included bathroom spigots that offered hot, cold and salt water. Glenn Miller performed each day at lunchtime in the mess hall. Two thousand young women volunteered as dancing partners or hostesses for the USO. Large dances were held in the Municipal Auditorium (now Boardwalk Hall), which ultimately led to hundreds of marriages between soldiers and local women.

This was the Atlantic City that Fred Noyes Jr. returned to after being wounded in France. The England General Hospital was his home for six months. And it was here, in the highly charged wartime atmosphere, that Fred and Ethel came to know each other.

Many women who lived in the area became Gray Ladies, volunteer nursing assistants to the Red Cross. Bertha Lingelbach recalled, "I volunteered for the Red Cross, and we used to take the fellows out on the boardwalk in their wheelchairs. Ethel never did that. The first time I was there, there was this heavyset fellow, Jack. He had lost both of his legs, and my brother Ev carried him on his back. I will never forget that. I have a picture somewhere of when Jack came back, and he was skating on the lake with his artificial legs."

Ethel was not a Gray Lady; in fact, she couldn't even stand the sight of blood, according to Bertha. One day there was an accident in front of their house in Oceanville. A bus had turned on its side in the road. There was a banging on the front door, and when they opened it, there was a girl with blood running down her face, saying, "Oh, no! Oh, no!" One look and Ethel ran up to the attic, not to be seen again. Bert had the girl come in and sit down, and she got a damp towel for her face.

Ethel sought out Fred when she learned he was in the England General Hospital. No longer a silly, foppish artist from Lower Bank, he came back from war a tough sergeant on crutches.

The first thing Ethel did was intervene on Fred's behalf to save his leg. The doctors wanted to amputate the badly injured limb, but Fred preferred a damaged leg to no leg at all. Ethel let the hospital staff know Fred was not a candidate for amputation, and that was the end of it. Fred instead wore a brace on his injured leg and remained in the hospital for six months. Ethel had a forceful way about her, and Fred liked this. They began to date, and from then on, things happened fast.

Fred's father had died on August 10, 1944. According to Lower bank neighbor Marge Downs Cavileer, Fred Sr. went to get gas that day with his friend Charlie Cavileer. The Mayor had a heart attack and died right at the gas station while Fritz was still in France. When Fred lost his father, he lost a good friend and a strong influence in his life, but Ethel was soon there to fill the gap.

Fred Noyes Sr.'s last will and testament was dated December 15, 1937, and witnessed by Fred Jr.'s good friend Walter K. Cavileer Jr. Fred Sr. bequeathed his estate as follows: "Two thirds to my son Fred W. Noyes, Jr. & one third to my wife Louisa K. Noyes and desire that they shall jointly administer my estate, and would advise that they consult old friends of mine for any advice they consider necessary." No dollar amount was indicated in the will as to the value of the estate. Some people believe the estate was worth upward of $100,000 and that Ethel had one eye on the money when she became interested in Fred.

Lois Lingelbach remembered, "You would look at Fred's father and think he doesn't have a cent. We used to see him marching down the Boardwalk with his hip boots on, old beat-up hunting jacket, hat pulled down over his head; he looked like some of the bag people. He used to go two or three times a week to see his broker at Advest Company to play the stock market. Great guy, he really was, a very brilliant man."

Bertha said, "Fritz did have some money. And Ethel wanted to get out of the home and get something started in business."

Ethel's friend and coworker at the Ration Board, Jane Betts Kubernus, knew even more about Ethel's dream.

"One day, before she married Fred, at the end of the war, we went for a ride and she said, 'I want to show you something.'

"We went up New York Road and we came to this old tumbled-down thing that had been Smithville Inn. I remember there was a fallen tree there and we got out and sat on it and I said to her, 'Ethel, why are we sitting on this tree and looking at this broken down building?'

"She said, 'Because some day I am going to make something here.'

"And I said, 'Oh yeah, Ethel, yeah, sure.'

"She said, 'Well, that is a dream I have and that is what I am going to do some day.'"

Another factor at play in Ethel and Fred's relationship was the atmosphere of camaraderie created by the war. To offset the tragedy and deprivation, there was a concerted effort to have fun. The Lingelbachs and some friends rented a cabin on Lily Lake, a pond profuse with white water lilies, just a mile north of the Lingelbach homestead on New York Road (Route 9). The cabin, built by the Works Progress Administration (WPA) as an office, had a big stone fireplace, and Ev Lingelbach barbecued whole pigs there. It was a place for the young people to get together, cook out, play music and dance. Jane Betts Kubernus said, "We spent every weekend at the cabin. When we weren't entertaining the fellows from England General Hospital, we just went there and had fun. We washed our hair in the lake."

Mamie Stone, Egg Harbor City postmistress, organized the weekend events for the soldiers. An ample woman with white hair pulled back from her lively face, Mamie arranged transportation for some amputees to go from Atlantic City to the cabin for a day's outing. Barbecue, music and the attention of pretty young women awaited the soldiers. Mamie's enthusiasm was contagious, and many young people came to the cabin for a good time. Sometimes Ethel's parents, Chris and Caroline Lingelbach, joined in. One photograph shows Fred standing between Caroline and Ethel, an arm casually around the shoulder of each woman, like he's already one of the family.

The mood during the fall of 1944 and the spring of 1945 was intense, heady and full of hope. The war was nearing its end. The economy was thriving, and there was opportunity everywhere.

Fred visited Ethel at the Rations Board and in the Lingelbach home, and he spent time at the cabin on Lily Lake. He was funny, artistic and garrulous, and he and Ethel got along well. No one else understood the attraction, however.

Fred's mother, Louisa, did not care for Ethel, but Fred didn't take her objections seriously. He had a mind of his own. Ethel's family and friends were mystified. Fred and Ethel's backgrounds were dissimilar, as were their personalities. She was a take-charge kind of person who knew what she wanted and what she expected of others. Bright and self-educated, Ethel was an ambitious woman. Fred, on the other hand, was easygoing, "a regular old shoe sort of person, not outgoing," Bertha observed. He did not appear to have a master plan for his life, other than to draw, paint and enjoy himself. Indeed, Fred would never get in the way of Ethel's plans. Bert attests, "Well, I don't know how to describe it; they were entirely different." In the end, this balance may have been a key to the enduring chemistry of their relationship.

Once Fred and Ethel decided to get married, they didn't waste any time. Romance was conspicuously absent from Fred's account of the marriage proposal. "What are you doin' tonight? Do you want to get married?" he asked. Apparently having no other plans, Ethel's response was "Yeah," and that was the sum of it.

The Lingelbach family was taken by surprise. The haste and absence of planning around the wedding was hard to understand; Bert called it the $64,000-dollar question. She said, "I didn't know they were going to be married that night, and I was supposed to stand up for them!" Jane and a few other friends found out just before it happened. "We all jumped into some sort of nice clothes and went over to see them get married."

The quiet marriage took place on March 21, 1945, in the small chapel at St. Andrews Lutheran Church in Atlantic City in front of family and a few friends. Although Ethel had sewn dresses for Jane Kubernus and her wedding party, she was unconcerned with what she would wear at her own wedding. Fred was in uniform. After the ceremony, the small group went back to the Lingelbach farm for champagne and sandwiches.

Whatever it was that brought them together at the close of World War II, and no matter what others thought, for Fred and Ethel, the marriage was what they wanted. And there was no point in waiting.

Fred on the beach in Longport with his parents, Fred Sr. and Louisa Bond Noyes, early 1920s. *Courtesy of Richard Lovett III.*

Right: Fred, an art student at the Pennsylvania Academy of the Fine Arts, Philadelphia, circa 1928. *Courtesy of the Noyes Museum of Art.*

Below: Fred, self-portrait at age twenty, painted in oils, 1925. *Courtesy of the Noyes Museum of Art.*

Above: Ethel, almost three years old, with her brother Everett, circa 1913. *Courtesy of Bertha Lingelbach.*

Left: Ethel in fourth grade, Pleasantville school, circa 1920. *Courtesy of Bertha Lingelbach.*

Fred in training at Fort Dix, New Jersey, 1941. *Courtesy of Bertha Lingelbach.*

Left: Ethel, thirty-one, manager of the Rations Board at Commercial Bank on Philadelphia Avenue in Egg Harbor City in 1942. *Courtesy of Bertha Lingelbach.*

Below: Ethel's parents, Christopher and Caroline Lingelbach, visiting their son Henry (Hap) at the medical corps in Albany, New York, 1942. *Courtesy of Bertha Lingelbach.*

Top: The log cabin on Lily Lake, across the lake from the Noyes Museum. Mamie Stone (center with white hair) organized transportation for the soldiers to come from the England General Hospital (Chalfonte-Haddon Hall, now Resorts Casino and Hotel) in Atlantic City to the cabin for cookouts and entertainment with local girls. Behind Mamie, clockwise: Ethel; Ethel's parents, Chris and Caroline Lingelbach; and Fred, 1945. *Courtesy of Bertha Lingelbach.*

Bottom: At the log cabin, *left to right:* Egg Harbor City postmistress Mamie Stone, Ethel, Fred and Ethel's mother, Caroline Lingelbach. *Courtesy of Bertha Lingelbach.*

Fred and Ethel's first house at 309 Church Street, Absecon, where they lived in the early '50s for about five years. *Author photo.*

Smithville Inn, about the time Ethel started to dream about making something out of it, circa 1940. *Historic Smithville Inns, Incorporated Annual Report 1973.*

Chapter 5

PARTNERS IN ARTS AND ANTIQUES

The sudden wedding left little time for Fred and Ethel to plan what would happen next. Ethel had a room of her own in the Lingelbach home, so the simplest solution was to stay there for a while. With his easygoing nature, Fred fit right in.

Almost immediately, Ethel developed health problems and had to undergo a hysterectomy. There was no longer a choice whether to have children. Ethel would never be a mother; her enormous energy would be channeled elsewhere. Without children to demand time, attention, love and financial resources, Fred and Ethel would create a life that revolved around their business partnership.

Fred was discharged from the army in April 1945, just one month after the wedding. The Atlantic City Racetrack in McKee City, about fourteen miles from Oceanville, was under construction. Bob Hope, Frank Sinatra and six nationally known bandleaders were among the stockholders. The track was an exciting place that attracted all types, from the working-class wage earner to the high-class horse owner. Whether standing at the rail or sitting in a box, the adrenaline of the gambling and the horses' hooves pounding around the dirt track kept the energy level high. Fred got a job there. As Ethel's sisters remembered it, he was a handy man; his job had to do with maintenance and construction.

Fred loved to eat. Ethel's mother complained he often ate so much and so fast that she was certain he hadn't tasted anything. As a joke, she once put a piece of cardboard between two slices of bread and packed it with the rest of his sandwiches to take to work. He never mentioned it. Though Fred was trim in his early years, "he would eat everything in sight," remembered Bertha. His parents were never heavy, nor was the Lingelbach family. But food became a constant issue in Fred and Ethel's relationship. She ate sparingly while he tended to indulge in double portions.

For a little while, Fred and Ethel lived in the unheated cabin at Lily Lake with only an outside toilet. They also stayed with Fred's mother in Lower Bank. This was a short stay and probably not a pleasant one. Lois said, "If they lived out at Lower Bank, I can assure you it would have been no more than a month that Ethel lived out there!" Next-door neighbor Marge Downs Cavileer recounted, "Mrs. Noyes didn't really want Fred to marry Ethel. She didn't like her, never liked her." In turn, the Lingelbach sisters didn't have much good to say about Louisa. They remembered her as being hoity-toity and living in the past. She had come from Philadelphia wealth and never let you forget it. In society, you never cleaned your plate; it was low class. It drove Ethel crazy when Louisa left little bits of this and that on her plate, even if she was hungry.

Within a few months, Fred and Ethel bought their first home. Using part of Fred's inheritance, they purchased a bungalow near the center of Absecon at 309 Church Street for about $4,000.

The war came to an end in September 1945. The Ration Board closed later that year, and Ethel never worked for anyone else again.

She had spent many hours with her Aunt Daisy, scouring the countryside for antiques and making contacts with other collectors. But it was her father, Chris Lingelbach, who had the strongest and deepest influence on her. Marge Conover was married to Daisy's son Floyd, and they spent a lot of time with Ethel and Fred. Marge reflected on Chris Lingelbach, "I think it was the type of down-to-earth person he was; his whole being was earthy. He was a gardener, a farmer; he was not well educated but he was an earthy man. Ethel was always interested in earthy things like old buildings and artifacts. And she loved the recipes that had been handed down.

"She was a lot more interested than most people who just live around things," continued Marge. "They don't see them; they just take them for granted because they have always lived in the area. Ethel was interested to the extent that she wanted to investigate and really go into the historical end of things. I don't know what her final goal was; I think one thing led to another. She was able to take advantage of her contacts, and she appreciated her father for what he was and his values."

Ethel researched the Lingelbach family history. She joined the Daughters of the American Revolution and studied the family tree. She explored the Strickland branch and the Lenape connection. Always an avid reader, she educated herself in her favorite subjects: antiques and the history and folklore of South Jersey. She read books and magazines and interrogated shopkeepers and other antiques buffs. Then she put her education into action.

Ethel had a good eye and good timing. Her sister Bert recalled, "I would be looking for something, and I would have to look and look. Without even looking, she would walk right into it, just knowing it was right. When she started the antiques business, no one was looking for them, and you could pick things up for nothing. Now it would cost you a fortune." Lois added, "Ethel was a business woman. You know, the average person around here didn't know what they had in their attic, and they weren't really interested."

"We went around to different houses and asked if there was anything we could buy or sell," said Fred. He and Ethel developed an approach to buying antiques that combined bargaining and playacting. They would be in an antiques shop browsing, and Ethel would say in a voice that could be easily overheard, "Oh, Fred, I really love this." Fred would go over to the owner and say, "How much is it?" And no matter what the response, Fred would reply, "Good God, that's too much." They would go back and look around some more, and Ethel would say, "Oh, Fred, this is really nice and I really want this." Fred would say, "Oh, no. That's a ridiculous price." Then, "Oh, Fred, look at this, wouldn't this look good in such and such a place?" Response: "No. That's way too much money." After a bit more of this, Fred would go over to the shop owner and say, "Excuse me, my wife really wants that. Can you do any better on that? What's the best you can do?" By this time, the salesperson was feeling sorry for Ethel and would lower the price.

Lois, not yet married, accompanied Fred and Ethel to antiques shows in New England and Pennsylvania in the late 1940s. Ethel spent a lot of time quizzing other dealers to learn more about antiques. The Noyeses had a booth of their own, and she and Fred honed their bargaining skills on the selling side as well.

Collecting and trading antiques soon led to a need for more space. They bought the house behind their bungalow that fronted on New Jersey Avenue, the main shopping street in Absecon. City Hall, the Absecon National Bank, a butcher, a five and dime store, a liquor store, an insurance agency and several other stores lined the street.

Fred used one room in the 310 New Jersey Avenue house to repair and refinish the furniture to be sold. He also set up a studio and sometimes painted with other artists. One artist was Violet Mason, an Absecon resident married to Dr. James Mason III. Violet's granddaughter Cindy Mason-Purdie recalled, "My grandmother and Fred always admired each other's painting ability. They were both serious about their painting; I see a lot of similarities. They painted still life and flowers and had a strong sense of design. There are some things I think she painted with Fred. They had an over-the-edge sense of humor, more Fred than my grandmother. Fred more than her, I think, because he was such a jolly-looking guy."

Ethel was quick to take advantage of available family and friends to help her with her business. She shared her excitement and vision and made it fun to work with her. She had a good sense of timing when it came to getting help. Jane Betts, Ethel's friend from the Ration Board, lost her husband in 1948. Jane said, "My marriage didn't last long, so I went back home to live with my parents in Absecon. Then Ethel says to me, 'You have nothing better to do; come work with me in my antiques shop.' So I did. I used to go antiquing with her. I remember crawling through attics in Leeds Point and Smithville and every other place you could think of. We would just go and knock on doors! Well, she knew a lot of those families; she was born and raised there."

Fred was also an avid collector, but he had his own interests stimulated by years living on the Mullica River. He was not a hunter, but he had lived among hunters and he came to appreciate duck decoys. The hunters carved working decoys that would float on the water and look realistic enough to decoy a flight of ducks into shooting range. When Fred started his collection in the late 1940s, there were only a couple other collectors in the area.

Oceanville native Milton Heinzer was thirteen years old when he first began to walk the marshes after a storm and pick up decoys that had washed in. He piled the decoys in the basket of his bike and pedaled to Fred's. Fred paid him three dollars apiece for the decoys.

Over time, decoys became a collector's item. By 2006, at an auction in Easton, Maryland, a black-bellied plover decoy carved by Elmer Crowell was sold "after an intense bidding battle" for the record price of $830,000.

The Noyeses' antiques shop was on a main street but not in the commercial section. Fred said, "I made the mistake of putting a sign out, 'Antiques for Sale,' and the Absecon big shots came around and said, 'You can't sell in this territory. This is residential.' I told them to shove it. A guy spends four years in the army and gets busted up, and they won't let him have an antiques shop in his basement."

This forced the Noyeses to relocate their business to the most traveled thoroughfare in Absecon, the White Horse Pike (also called Route 30), which runs east and west, parallel to the railroad tracks between Atlantic City and Philadelphia. They set up shop in an old hotel that offered more space and provided higher visibility for the business. But there were drawbacks: "There was no water, no toilet. If you had to take a leak, you had to come home." Fred taught art in a back room. "I had a class of about ten to twenty kids. I was teaching privately and otherwise at the time. The kids had little beanies with pinwheels on top, and I said to myself I'd rather starve to death than teach those little brats." Fortunately, as the art classes dwindled off, the antiques business thrived. "We sat there for ninety-two days, I think it was, before we made a sale. We were so close to giving up, it was funny. Then a guy came over from the Atlantic City Boardwalk and bought $300 to $400 worth of stuff. My God, we almost died."

The Noyeses expanded their knowledge and their business by forging relationships with other people who were interested in antiques. Jack and Margo Clayton were two people who came into their world at this time and remained for many years. Jack's mother knew about the Noyeses' shop in Absecon, but it was the Williamsburg Forum that brought the Claytons and the Noyeses together. A Colonial revival movement was growing in the United States. John D. Rockefeller started the restoration in Williamsburg in 1926, and places like the Shelburne Museum in New York State and historic Deerfield and Sturbridge in Massachusetts were being developed into historic sites. The first Antiques Forum, held in Colonial Williamsburg, Virginia, in 1949, was a weeklong educational event that attracted dealers and collectors to hear experts lecture on furniture, paintings and early American objects. They also came to compare and share information. The growing interest in antiques boosted by the prosperous postwar economy created a mood of excitement. The Noyeses, Jack Clayton and another couple, Mae and Ezra Bell, met at the Forum and quickly became friends when they realized they were all from the Atlantic City area. Jack Clayton remembered, "Fred and I were both graduates of the Philadelphia College for Arts, and he went to the Academy. We knew some of the same artists and antiques dealers. Fred and Ethel were both knowledgeable. Fred did a lot of furniture restoring; he would have on an apron, a paintbrush and cleaning bands."

When Ethel learned the Claytons worked at Norman's, a ladies' ready-to-wear shop in Atlantic City, a business relationship developed. Margo Clayton recollected, "To create a background for the fashion display, we would borrow a few antiques and make a vignette. Not a complete room, but a low boy and a chair and the mannequin would stand in front of it. We would put a sign in the window that the antiques were from Ethel and Fred Noyes of Absecon."

Jack elaborated, "Ethel would come in to buy something, and she would say, 'Oh, you know I have this nice chest I think would look good in the window.' Then we would do cotton dresses or wool skirts or something and actually build the window around the chest." Thus the Noyeses got gratuitous and prominent advertising on the main street in Atlantic City.

Fred and Ethel's friendship with the Bells was to have an even more significant impact. Mae and Ezra Bell were co-owners of the Morton Hotel in Atlantic City along with Paul and Alice Cope. They also operated the Morton Motor Ranch, a motel with riding horses on the White Horse Pike in Absecon. The Bells were older than the Noyeses and had achieved much that Ethel aspired to. Mae had an antiques shop in the Morton Hotel and often traveled to Europe to buy inventory. Ezra was an astute businessman with extensive hotel, restaurant and customer service experience.

By now Fred and Ethel owned four properties in Absecon: their home on Church Street, the house on New Jersey Avenue, the antiques shop on the White Horse Pike and the former Odd Fellows Hall, also on Church Street. Odd Fellows Hall was a handsome, classical building of simple lines, with an apartment in the rear. It was here that Fred moved his mother. Louisa was frail and often unwell. Lois Lingelbach said, "I remember one time they went down to see Fred's mother on Church Street. She had a cute little apartment in the back of that house. They went to check on her, you know they did everyday, just to make sure she was all right. Well they both thought she was dead! She was passed out; her little bottle was empty. But she had to have that medication." Louisa revived, but she continued to carry little bottles of "medication" in her purse and take nips from time to time.

Ethel's passion for acquiring real estate continued to grow. It was time to begin the realization of the dream she had shared with her friend Jane when they sat on a log and looked at a tumbledown building on New York Road.

The casual passerby could easily miss the Smithville Inn in 1950. The four-room building was abandoned, battered by the elements and overgrown with bushes and weeds. To Ethel's astute eye, the obscure structure was a treasure waiting to be discovered. The Inn had three assets she valued. First, it was architecturally pleasing. Second, the building had historic interest. And third, it was well located on New York Road, or Route 9, which was then the main north–south artery in New Jersey connecting New York City to Cape May.

Others might have disagreed about the location. Six miles north of Absecon, and even farther from Atlantic City, Smithville was not a center of activity. Ethel believed the action would come to her. Rome was not built in a day, nor was Williamsburg. She did not worry about obstacles. She chose instead to think, to talk and to work toward making her vision a reality. And she had Fred with her every step of the way.

The colorful history of the Smithville Inn ignited Ethel's imagination and fueled her ardor for her work. James Baremore, an adventurer and businessman from Philadelphia, came to South Jersey shortly after the War for Independence with his partner, Peter Turner. They moved to Smithville, where they married cousins, Eunice and Mary Leeds. Baremore purchased land from John Smith and built the original Inn, a one-room, brick-lined, cedar clapboard building, in 1787. It stood on the stagecoach route between Coopers Landing, now Camden, about fifty miles to the west, and Leeds Point a few miles east. It was the only tavern in the area licensed to serve Yankee Rum. The drink came in pewter cups for three cents. Turner eventually moved on, but Baremore, a salty character and spinner of yarns, stayed. He bought land on Brigantine beach and commuted on a crude ferry from Leeds Point. Baremore's son-in-law, Isaac Smith, purchased the Inn and acreage for $400 in 1819. With his wife, Sarah, Isaac operated the Inn, managed his large farm and raised a family of thirteen children. His son Henry Smith ran the business until 1865.

In its heyday in the late 1700s and early 1800s, the Inn was a welcome respite for stagecoach passengers. The stage left Cooper's Ferry at 3:00 a.m. and made its first stop at Long-a-Coming, now Berlin. It proceeded along the trail, originally made by the Native Americans and better suited to walking than wagon wheels, through the towns of White Horse, Waterford Works, Hammond's Town (Hammonton), Batsto, Pleasant Mills and Port Republic and arrived at the Smithville Inn by evening. The coach ride on hardwood seats over rutted sand roads and through rushing streams was uncomfortable, dirty and sometimes scary. There were wildcats, bears and panthers in the forest until the late eighteenth century. The weary traveler was ready for a cup or more of grog and a hot meal upon arriving at Smithville.

Things changed, however, when the Camden-Atlantic Railroad was built in 1854 connecting Camden to Absecon. Smithville was bypassed. Travelers preferred the more comfortable rail cars, and the stagecoaches became infrequent. Another setback was the growing popularity of Brigantine Island and bathing in the Atlantic Ocean. A rail line spur was built to Brigantine Island through the town of Oceanville, and Smithville lost its post office. Parts of the inn were disassembled by James Baremore's grandson, Henry D. Smith, and taken to Brigantine to build a hotel there in 1857. Only the brick-lined room, the fireplace room and the two chambers above remained. Eventually, even that was abandoned.

Ethel envisioned what others could not see. "It was nothing more than an unpainted, dilapidated four-room house, but I wanted to make this old place good again," she said. Next she had to convince Fred to join in the project. He said, "No, I don't want any part of that little old dump." But eventually he gave in. He loved Ethel's verve.

The Noyeses partnered with the Bells to buy the property in May 1951. Ethel and Mae forged the original modest concept: a lunchroom and tearoom with antiques for sale. Fred wrote later, "Ethel and Mrs. Ezra Bell were the ones that really got it started. Ethel and I had about $6,000 and Mrs. Bell, or Mae, put $20,000 into it." The initial outlay for the abandoned building and seven acres was $3,972.11. That is an exact figure, neatly entered in a notebook that Ethel kept. Along with it are other figures: electrician, $592.00; furnishings, $2,476.50; and "furnishings temporarily considered a loan," $800.50. They borrowed $1,000.00 more, and with a total outlay of $9,841.11, Smithville Inn was back in business.

Items that were not entered in Ethel's notebook were sweat equity and perseverance. It was an overwhelming investment. Years later, Fred told the *Press of Atlantic City* reporter Ed Hitzel, "My wife forced me into buying the old house up there and making an antique shop out of it. It was $4,000. I can remember that. I wrote them a check for $100 down payment. It was just a little old dump. And we bought it and fixed it up. I really didn't want any part of it. I told her I'd work for her. I took the job as dishwasher for nothing. I was dishwasher there for nine years, that's how long it took to get over the hump."

Chapter 6

ETHEL LEADS, FRED BALANCES THE ACT

We weren't too proud to do whatever had to be done…it was our love for this region that kept us going.
—Ethel Noyes

Our History of Smithville Inn
By Fred W. Noyes Jr.

This is the story of Smithville Inn as we grew up with it these 16 years from 1952–1968. First of all my wife and I bought the old Inn that was run down and grown up with weeds, vines and brushes and trees… for this we paid $3,500.00 including 4½ acres of more woods, tin can dumps, trash heaps and bottle heaps. I can remember when we were tying white rags on trees around the old house to keep the bulldozer from taking them away with all the brush. Then we cleaned up the bulldozed area by burying trash, bottles and tin cans, deep into the ground and into the very deep well that used to be in front of the old Inn. The lake as we all see it today was a little run you could step over running through the middle of a cranberry spun.

This was just a starter—then came the headaches and heartaches. We brought in our carpenters and started to work on the Inn. This was really something, and may I say here and now, if anyone who reads this is thinking about restoring an old house, you had better be plenty rugged and have plenty of good liquor to keep up your courage, because you will run into many a day when you feel like giving it back to the Indians and that is where your bottle of good V.O. comes in handy.

Well, after many days of hard work and trying to get the men to do things the way you want it done, some of which you will have to do over and over again—say in about a year you see things quickly fall into place after searching out wallpapers, flowering curtain material, etc. The expense of restoring the Inn was so great, the cost of buying it for $3,500.00 was nothing. But after it was restored and we had spent so much money on it, we wanted to get our money back.

So we decided to sell antiques and sell sandwiches—cake and coffee and stuff for women looking for antiques. We used a back room for a kitchen, or so called, and we hired a girl from down the road called Viola Conover. Viola was a fine cook and a fine person, so we hired her to make pies— coffee and toast and small stuff.

Then I was the guy that worked in the kitchen. My wife "Ethel," God Bless Her, hired me to wash dishes and clean the floors and all the kitchen work such as run errands, cut grass, rake the parking lot, sweep, trim trees, take care of the trash and garbage, etc., etc. All this was for the small wages of +000.00. Oh, yes, and all I could eat. And I did eat—such as 6–8 eggs, 10 pieces of buttered toast, and I mean buttered, and a pot of coffee—just for breakfast.

My wife "Ethel" was the boss and handled all the money and front end, which was a big job. In the Reception Room, which was the entrance to the Smithville Inn, which we named it, we sold jellies, bread, cigarettes, cigars, etc. We had a cigar box for a cash register. It was a beautiful little room with a real old antique desk which at that time, now 18 years ago, cost $250 to $300. Today as I am writing, the same desk would be worth at least $1,500 or more.

Well anyhow, we were started. We began to need a refrigerator, so we brought ours from home, our freezer we brought from home and a coffee maker also. Then we needed a sink to wash dishes and pans, etc. So we invested in a soda fountain, zinc type deal, and a gas range. At that we were lucky because the gas line ran just as far as our Inn because just across the street was competition: a little restaurant called the "Green Top Restaurant" run by a couple, very nice German people. In those days we would look out the window at each car that came by and wonder if they were going to stop or not.

Well, I forgot to tell you that Ethel and Mrs. Ezra Bell were the ones that really got it started. Ethel and I had about $6,000.00 and Mrs. Bell, or May as we called her, put $20,000.00 into it.

Then someone said, why don't you try a hot dinner in the evening. We talked about—we would need ranges, broilers and a cook or chef—here we go! Mr. Bell said we wouldn't do 10 dinners a year. So we decided, or they did, to do it and we bought all we needed and found a chef— Gus Howelett's from Absecon—an old man of fine past experience at the Waldorf and Jack Dempsey's in New York City.

Well, I never knew a chef needed so damn much stuff to cook with. There seemed to be no end in sight. But we went along. By the way, our first tables and chairs we bought cost us $2 each, and we still are using some.

So came the big nite and believe me, to us it was a big nite. We then seated about 44 people and we had the place filled. Remember, no liquor, just food. So the customers brought their own liquor and if four people brought a 5th for dinner, they thought they should drink it. And they usually did. Many customers, most of which were our good, good friends, would bring me out a drink and help me mash potatoes. I remember now the pot was big and I used to put the pot on the floor and pound the hell out of them. Lew and Off used to come into the kitchen with a big drink for me and help me mash the potatoes, while I would have to run down to the cellar and open 4 orders of clams or oysters. Then I would cuss—why the hell do they have to eat oysters just now?

We had three waitresses who used to carry their trays out in front of them and some of them are still here—God Bless Them. I used to give them hell—smack them on the ass and they loved it.

One nite we had a group of fellows; about six came in and this was a hell of a deal—six men at once. Well everything went swell until they got a few drinks under their belts and started to kid with our little country waitress who was not used to such men of the world. So when it came to dessert, one asked for Brown Betty, and they picked it up from there and the next said I'll take a Blonde Betty. The next said I'll take a Red Head. All the time our little country waitress was getting more and more shook up and embarrassed. So the next guy ordered, "Well, let's see, I'll just take Betty, or how about you, little girl?"

Well just about that time, all hell broke loose. The waitress came running thru the kitchen crying and telling me about these guys insulting her and she never stopped going. I can still see her yet, running across the back lawn and up the road to home. That was the last of her.

All the time Ethel was wondering what happened and started to give me hell thinking I had hurt the little girl's feelings.

But all in all the first nite was one to remember and at this time I want to thank all those good friends—and you all know who you are—for coming in and starting us on one hell of an adventure. Come what may here, we were started—and how!

Ethel used to cook and clean and tend the front and the dining room, handle all the money and do all of the office work. We used to pay in cash then; we had about 10 employees. So after everyone was gone for the nite, Ethel and I would clean the kitchen and scrub the floor, take inventory of goods in iceboxes—pies, etc. and make up our order for the next day. Sometimes this would be 1 or 2 o'clock before we would get home and then back again at 5:30 or 6 o'clock in the morning to go to market and haul ice, clams, oysters, etc. Then we used to prepare our vegetables for the chef and cook the shrimp. In those days we had our preparation room in the basement, now used for water pumps. Then the chef needed a helper, so we hired a girl who cooked for a family of six people.

Well, by this time we were starting to do a little business—maybe 20 people a day. We then had an office upstairs in one little room where we used to rest when we could and another room upstairs we used as a sitting room.

But then came Thanksgiving and we got overloaded. So we also fed people upstairs on Thanksgiving, using our office and the extra room. I can still remember one very important man that was seated in the second floor room saying, "Hell, if I wanted to eat in an attic, I could have eaten in my own." This hurt us very much because we were trying so hard to do a good job—and till this day, 16 years later, I still don't like that guy.

But lots of folks used to enjoy it. In fact, Mr. Kelly was at the racetrack and used to have little parties in this same room. This was Grace Kelly's father, now Princess Grace.

Well, we started to grow. I remember the first room we put on was a screened in porch to seat 14 more people. And some of our customers would say, if you get too big we won't come out anymore; we like it just the way it is. But each month the mortgage had to be paid and each week wages had to be dealt out

Here ends the story that Fred wrote in his own hand. There must have been more pages, for there is no period after "dealt out," but they are nowhere to be found. (Fred's writing appears courtesy of Tony and Fran Coppola, Possessors of Smithville Inn.)

The renovated Smithville Inn opened in May 1952 and served 847 guests that first year. In hindsight, there should have been a drum roll and the pulling back of great velvet curtains on the stage, for Smithville was to become the setting of an unfolding drama set in motion by a visionary entrepreneur and her supportive artist husband.

Major improvements were always in process. The "little run you could step over" was dug out and filled with water. Ethel honored her Native American heritage by naming it Lake Meone after the last princess of the Leni-Lenape.

The restaurant seating increased. "We bought tables and chairs out of a junkyard. Then they started to holler about liquor so we went out and bought a liquor license for $10,000," Fred said. Realizing there was a good profit to be made, Fred was ready to take on bartending.

"My first bar was a card table, and I had a bucket of ice on the floor—now this is the God's honest truth—and the first guy wanted a whiskey sour. I told the waitress, 'Now you go back and tell him I want to talk to him.' I told him I didn't know how to make a whiskey sour. I told him, 'You show me, and I'll give you the first drink for nothing.' That's how I learned to be a bartender."

The partnership with the Bells came to an end when Fred and Ethel bought them out. Some people say it was because the Bells were Quaker and Ezra Bell would not let Mae work there once they started serving alcohol. This is questionable because alcoholic drinks were served at the Bell's Morton Hotel in Atlantic City. The Bells had been basically financial partners while the Noyeses were the working partners.

The Bells had made a strong imprint on the business in a short time. Many people who knew Ezra Bell and Ethel Noyes thought they were very much alike. They both thought fast, knew what they wanted and expected it to be done yesterday. Later, Ezra would refer to Ethel as a "tough one" and hard to work for. But Ethel had learned many of her demanding standards from Ezra himself. Ethel also benefited from her relationship with Mae, a businesswoman who was smart, soft-spoken and a go-getter, all traits Ethel emulated.

From the beginning, they stressed customer service. "The secret is making a person feel like a million bucks," said Fred. "And know their names. 'Good evening, Mr. Smith. It's good to see you. We'll have your table ready. I think you'll like it.'"

The postwar economy was booming. It was the perfect time to enlarge the Inn. Ethel was unstoppable. Once an addition was started, she would move onto the next project, multitasking decades before the phrase was coined. Her vision moved one step ahead of her projects, and the people around her ran to keep the pace. In this whirlwind of activity, there was no such thing as a job description or contract. Everyone did whatever was necessary to get the job done. The first place Ethel looked for help was to her family. She would have loved to have her brothers, Hap and Ev, in the business. As the oldest child, she was comfortable in the position of boss and would happily have taken charge of her siblings. Ev had worked in the Philadelphia Naval Yard and Hap had served as a medic in World War II. Both went into the construction business after the war. But when the building boom began in Florida, they headed south.

The first to become involved in the business was Lois, the baby in the Lingelbach family. In 1951, she married Bob Muller, a former classmate at Pleasantville High School. Bob had enlisted in February 1943 and completed his high school diploma in the navy. After the war, he pursued a mechanical engineering degree at the University of Virginia and North Carolina State. Bright, handsome and energetic, Bob left college for a job with the Exxon Company in Venezuela in 1948. Lois also forged a career. After working in the Naval Air Station during the war, she was a bookkeeper at Freihofer's Bakery and then got a job in the accounting department at Sun Oil in Philadelphia. Through all this their romance thrived, and after their wedding, Lois went to Venezuela with Bob. She worked for Creole, a subsidiary of Exxon, in the pregnancy relief program. Her job was to substitute for native workers who needed time off to have their babies.

Fred and Ethel were having trouble keeping up with their fast-growing business. Some nights they kept such long hours that Fred slept in the car at the Inn. Venezuela was not too far away to reach for help when needed. Ethel convinced Bob and Lois that opportunities abounded with their Smithville enterprise and that the Mullers would be richly rewarded. So the newlyweds came back from South America, bought a house in Absecon and began to work at the Inn.

When asked what she did that first year, Lois responds, "Everything. I was a receptionist, waitress, hostess and cashier. Whatever was needed."

Sometimes busloads of visitors stopped by the Inn without notice. The flurry of activity that ensued kept everyone running. If they ran out of food, Fred dashed over to Oyster Creek, a bayfront restaurant just a couple miles down the road, to buy clams and steaks to bring back to feed the hungry guests. Lois kept up this pace even when she became pregnant. She worked right up until her first child was born.

One of Bob's jobs was to open a bar with Fred in the new Captain's Quarters in the Inn. With the help of *Mr. Boston's Bar Guide*, they stocked the bar and began serving drinks.

Both Bob and Lois devoted themselves day and night to the growing business, but long hours combined with unfulfilled promises caused them to become frustrated and discouraged. Exxon was still courting Bob, and when their daughter was eighteen months old, he went back to Venezuela to work for his former employer. Lois followed shortly after with baby Christine in early 1955.

Ethel's other sister, Bertha, was recruited gradually. Bert, as she was called by friends and family, had gone to work for Freihofer's Bakery in 1935 in Atlantic City after graduating from high school. It was one of the largest businesses in the area, and the summers were especially demanding. Bert liked the pace at Freihofer's, where she worked on a Comptometer, a high-speed calculating and adding machine. She stayed with Freihofer's for nineteen years and then went to work at Seaview Country Club, an exclusive private club with two nationally known golf courses. Seaview was just a stone's toss from the Lingelbach homestead on New York Road.

Bert would leave her job at Seaview at 4:00 p.m., stop home to change her clothes and then go to the Inn at 5:00 p.m. She started as a receptionist, greeting customers as they arrived and working in the coatroom. As the business burgeoned, Ethel enticed her to join the staff full time. She utilized Bert's cashier skills and put her in the office upstairs to handle the money. Bert was family, and Fred and Ethel trusted her.

The number of employees grew rapidly, and so did Ethel's talents as a manager. She settled for nothing but the best from everyone. Standards were set and maintained so the customer could expect consistent high quality. The waiters' and waitresses' hands were inspected daily, palms up and palms down, for cleanliness and neatly groomed nails. Excessive makeup was not allowed, and hair need to be neatly coifed. For the men, long hair or facial hair was not permitted.

Presentation included carefully designed costumes. The waiters wore crisp white long-sleeved shirts, black bow ties and black vests. The waitresses wore white pinafore aprons over black dresses and tall starched white hats with narrow, black velvet ribbon bands around the crown in colonial American style. The staff were required to take their uniforms home every day to launder and press them to keep them looking fresh. This was particularly hard when the restaurant did not close until late at night.

Edna Marshall was one of the early employees. She heard about the job in 1953 from a friend who worked at the Inn. Edna lived in the town of Tuckerton, about ten miles north of Smithville on Route 9.

"So I went down on the bus to apply for a job the day that Lois and Bob's baby Chrissy was born. That was in September, and Mrs. Noyes called me the next week. I didn't know a thing about waitressing or drinks. Then my girlfriend quit to work for the electric company, so I blame her for making me work there for thirty-two years!" Edna may not have known a thing about waitressing, but Ethel knew talent when she saw it.

Edna Marshall was almost ninety years old when she told this story. She was one year older than Ethel, but even after thirty-two years of employment and twenty years of retirement, Edna still referred to her as "Mrs. Noyes." This title of respect was used by all the Smithville employees, including those who became close with the Noyeses. When Edna was hired at Smithville, there were seven other waitresses. The Inn had two little rooms, the Port Republic Room and the Red Room, and the larger Absegami Room had just been added.

Edna's work and career advancement was as rapid as the growth of the Inn itself. "I was a waitress for about four years, hostess about four years, then I was personnel director the rest of the time; hired and fired. It was growing. We didn't have any personnel department when I started there. After eight years, we couldn't do without one."

Because she worked her way up through the ranks, Edna knew what it took to do waitressing and hostessing. She knew how to deal with a demanding employer and customers who expected a supreme dining experience. Edna often took home the waitresses' aprons and hats to give them a starch or ironing touch up. The staff respected and liked her because she pulled no punches. She was a straight talker who admired Ethel's work ethic.

"I hope some of that rubbed off on me," said Edna. "I was a waitress and a hostess, and I was there in the evening. I worked six days. Mrs. Noyes would call me on a weekend and say, 'Edna, would you come down please, we're stuck and we need help.' So I would take a bus and go down there and open up a station and work as a waitress!

"One time she was sick in bed, and she called to chat. She wanted me and the manager at the Inn to come over. She was living back on Sooy Lane then. So we went over, and she said she wanted us to go to Paris, the produce distributor, and get fruit for the lobby at the Inn. She had a great big flat fruit bowl, a cake dish, and she wanted me to arrange the fruit on it. Well, I did, and I thought it was beautiful. Next day she came in and took it all apart and did it all over again!

"She was a perfectionist. She would look at something and say, 'Oh, it is lovely,' but then she would have to change one little thing. That is why she liked to talk to the carpenters. She knew exactly what she wanted. If she came by and I had put something here, she would move it there. All the kids, they didn't like it. It didn't bother me. She was my boss, and she knew what she wanted, and like I said, I certainly hope some of it rubbed off on me."

Edna recalled, "She was good to me; they often took me places. She and I would go on trips to antique shows. She took me down to the beauty parade, the Miss America Pageant Parade in Atlantic City. We had rolling chairs on the Boardwalk, and I stayed at their motel overnight. Their motel at Smithville had about eight rooms. They took me out to dinner at Seaview, and they took the five- and ten-year employees to Philadelphia for shows.

"There was no pension. She was always going to, going to. We had health benefits, and then she would cancel that. She was supportive of me though.

"I knew everybody," said Edna. "I gave them their paychecks. At one time, we had five hundred employees.

"Mrs. Noyes enjoyed working with men and having meetings with men. Bob Haviland, carpenter and head of maintenance, Floyd Conover, the painter and the plumbers. She liked talking with men, she didn't like girl talk. All business. Mr. Noyes would sit there and she would say something and he would say, 'We've come a long way, baby.'"

Not everyone could deal with Ethel. She once instructed a hostess, who was dressed in a long dress with velvet trim and a colonial bonnet, to sweep the bricks in front of the Inn. "I wasn't hired to clean," declared the hostess as she stalked off the job. Without missing a beat, Ethel picked up the broom and did the job herself.

Edna knew how to handle Fred, who became increasingly rambunctious as the pretty waitress staff expanded and opportunities for teasing abounded. "I'll tell you what he did," said Edna, "and this is true, from the horse's mouth. He walked with a cane, and every time a girl went by he would lift the back of her skirt up with his cane. He sat in the kitchen on a great big stool, and he would call in orders and as the girls went by he just took his cane like this. One time he called me to come over to the Reception Hall. I went over and I went in and he says, 'How are you, fat ass?' and I kept right on going. People were looking at me; I never said a word to him. I just ignored him."

Early on, before they could afford to order flowers from a florist, Edna remembered Fred and Ethel walking along Old Port Road picking wild flowers to decorate the dining tables at the Inn. This was also before Ethel's days became so full that she didn't have time to smell a flower, let alone pick one. Only a few years later, Ethel would say, "I haven't heard a thing about Aunt Daisy lately. Edna, send her some flowers." This was the Aunt Daisy with whom Ethel had spent many happy hours driving through the South Jersey countryside, looking at old houses and antiques.

"Every year she built a new room on the Inn," recalled Edna, "I don't know how many rooms I helped open." The first addition was the Absegami Room, which more than doubled the dining area. Built in 1953 on the north side of the inn, the design carried out the early American theme with beamed ceilings, hardwood floors and a large brick fireplace at the far end of the room. It was a showplace for some of the antiques the Noyeses had collected. A Colonial portrait hung over the oak mantle, flanked by brass candlesticks. The walls were covered in handsome Schumacher paper, and curtains of matching fabric decorated the windows. Candles in sconces were mounted on the walls, and gently burning candles in pewter candlesticks stood on round and rectangular linen-covered tables, surrounded by captain-style chairs, to create a warm and welcoming atmosphere.

Looking down a row of tables with candlestick centerpieces, Ethel put her arm around the shoulders of a waitress, and with a tone of camaraderie, asked, "What could be done to make this look better?" The waitress cocked her head like Ethel's, so she too might have a keen surveyor's eye, and seeing a candlestick out of line, she would quickly suggest moving the offending candlestick an inch or two. Ethel then commended her. Rather than yell or criticize, Ethel had a way of eliciting the best from her employees.

A spacious reception room with a walk-in fieldstone fireplace was the next addition to the Inn. Then came new dining rooms that looked out over Lake Meone, where diners could watch families of ducks that lived on the pond. In the fall, the water reflected the burnt orange and gold leaves of the surrounding trees, and in winter, the black water contrasted sharply with the fresh snow. When the water froze, the surface gleamed white and attracted ice skaters.

The Galloway Room, named after the township in which the Inn is located, was originally a porch with a flagstone floor. It was enclosed for year-round dining and featured mullioned windows overlooking the lake. The atmosphere was nautical, with ship lanterns hanging from the ceiling beams and a carved whale and authentic harpoon mounted overhead on the fascia. The model of a tall-masted schooner stood on a spindled knee-wall dividing this room from the room behind it, the Captain's Quarters, a smaller dining room that featured the bar and connected to the kitchen.

From the Galloway Room, a ramp led down to the Great Bay Room. This addition was the largest yet and had floor-to-ceiling windows looking out to the lake. It was the perfect setting for sumptuous Sunday buffets and large parties, as well as gracious dining for many of the regulars. On the entrance side of the Inn, the smaller Mullica dining room and intimate Baremore Tavern completed the expansion.

At this time, rapid construction of interstate highways in the 1950s and 1960s changed the face of the American landscape. The Garden State Parkway was built from 1954 to 1957. It opened South Jersey to the more populated northern part of the state, as well as the New York metropolitan area and New England. From the west, the Atlantic City Expressway, constructed from 1962 to 1965, brought visitors from Philadelphia to the Jersey Shore in about an hour. This was an incredible boon for Smithville.

Affluence, the variety and availability of goods, the ability of advertisers to create a demand for these products and the growth of consumer credit all led to heightened buying power. The Noyeses' growing empire was in a position to benefit from the new shopping mania.

There was a small building across the street from the entrance to the Inn that was the perfect place to open a gift and antiques shop. The Noyeses purchased the structure, which had been known as Mrs. Ramsey's house, in 1955, made some minor renovations and opened it for business. Ethel recruited her mother, Caroline, to help out. Soon, however, personal tragedy struck.

Caroline and Chris Lingelbach had gone to St. Petersburg, Florida, in 1956 to visit Ev. Caroline, who suffered increasingly from heart problems, died suddenly of a heart attack while there. All the Lingelbachs mourned, especially Bertha, still single and extremely devoted to her mother.

About the same time, family friend Catherine White lost her husband. The Whites had been married nearly forty years when Herbert died. Catherine had never worked outside her home, but she said, "When my husband died, I needed work. So I went to the Inn. When I went there, Ethel's mother had just died. Ethel took me to the Gift Shop and said, 'I have just the place for you. This is yours; take care of it.'"

Catherine learned by doing, with a little help from Fred. "Fred was a great kidder. He used to come in my shop a lot and talk and laugh. A catalogue was made of all the gifts at one point. Ethel had someone come in and take pictures. Then people could place orders from the catalogue. Fred used to help me wrap and tie the packages to be shipped. It was hard work.

"They were always nice to me," said Catherine. "We would go overnight to New York. Mr. Noyes would drive. We would stay at a fine hotel for the weekend, and one time we ate at the Four Seasons Restaurant. I was treated well. We would shop all weekend at the Convention Center Gift Show."

Ethel got early entrance to the show because she placed substantial orders and she knew what she wanted. It only took a show or two before the dealers came to know Mrs. Noyes. Fred and Ethel ate at some of the city's finest restaurants. Ethel always kept her notepad and pencil with her and took notes on everything from menu selections to details of table décor.

When Ethel told Catherine, "This is yours," she meant it. "I could buy whatever I wanted at the gift show," said Catherine. "There was no budget. I bought what I wanted, and at the end of the day, she would pay and all the things would go to the shop. She trusted me. She knew that I never overbought. She knew I figured the amount that I needed. She never restricted me. Whatever I thought was nice. I decided how much was going to be charged for things from the show when we got back."

Ethel needed more stores, and she knew where to get them. She had traveled South Jersey's back roads, and she had come across abandoned old buildings that represented a lifestyle of days gone by. She was determined to save some of these structures and use them as shops.

The Red Barn was moved to Smithville in 1955. One of the few remaining early buildings in nearby Oceanville, the Red Barn dated back to the early 1800s and was constructed of pine board and cedar shingles. First the barn was moved to a location behind the Inn. Never afraid to change her mind if things could be improved, Ethel decided it would be better situated across the street next to the Gift Shop. Catherine White remembers there was an old-fashioned barn raising joined by many of the employees when the building was relocated. Large items of early Americana, such as grandfather clocks and rocking horses, were stocked in there.

In 1957, Cramer's General Store was moved from New Gretna, a small town about seven miles north on Route 9. The store was 115 years old and had sold everything from foodstuffs to yard goods, grain for farm animals, nails, garden seeds and fishing supplies. It had also been the gathering place for the villagers. Fred wrote to Sarah Ewing, a local historian who researched old buildings: "Sarah—This was our first venture in moving a building—it cost us $500 if I remember rightly, it must have been 13 or 14 years ago. This building is strictly all old and a very good example of an old country store. I remember when we opened it we used to burn coal in the little stove that was our only heat in the winter and we only opened the front room with only a couple of shelves full of merchandise and penny candy to sell."

Catherine helped open the General Store. She ran back and forth between there and her Gift Shop, working from 10:00 a.m. until 8:00 or 10:00 p.m. At first she took the money she made in her shops home at night. Then she heard there was a man in the area who was robbing people. Catherine became scared and arranged to take the day's receipts to Ethel at the Inn.

When she started in 1956, Catherine earned forty-five cents an hour plus commission on her sales, but the commission was taken away a couple years later. Mrs. Noyes, she said, needed the money for the expansion of the Inn.

Other things changed during the fourteen years Catherine worked for the Noyeses. "Later on when Smithville got so big, it almost got too big for them. We drifted apart," said Catherine. "We didn't go anywhere anymore. She was getting sick at this time. One time, Mr. Noyes was sick as well. One time Fred was in the shop. I called Ethel and told her that Fred didn't look too good. She dropped everything, rushed right over and took Fred to the hospital. He was in some kind of diabetic shock." Catherine continued to work for Fred and Ethel until she was seventy years old.

Sales in the shops increased as the Early American style became more popular. Markups on the merchandise were substantial, from 50 to 100 percent. When the Gift Shop and the General Store opened, the managers were responsible for everything. They paid rent, hired help, ordered, priced, displayed stock and did their own accounting.

In 1958, Catherine got some relief when Betty Loveland was hired to run Cramer's General Store. "It was fun," Betty said. "We worked like dogs for them. God, I used to stand there and put cement furniture together. I had to buy it, and when I got it, I had to put it together. I had to go shopping for this stuff because Ethel wanted it outside the Red Barn."

Betty was a forthright young woman, and at age ninety, she was still outspoken. She readily admits that her assertiveness is one of the reasons she lasted so long with the Noyeses. Betty and Edna Marshall were similar in the way they handled Fred and Ethel. "Yeah, we were. I didn't hide when they asked me questions." Like so many others who became Smithville employees, Betty had a friend who worked for the Noyeses.

"Doris Huntley said, 'Betty, you're not doing anything, why don't you come down here and get these people off my back.' So I went down with no idea of going to work, but there I stayed...I had to wear a long dress, you know, and bonnet. They told me they wanted someone to run the General Store. I didn't know from nothing, and they put me to work in the Gift Shop with Catherine. It was polish this, and polish the other thing. I had to make displays. I don't mean to run Catherine White down, but she was a lot older than I was and she wouldn't admit it. The Noyeses told us what they wanted. They were buying the stuff at this time, and we would set things up so they would sell. The Gift Shop had china and glassware, and it ended up with jewelry and all kinds of stuff. Catherine had to display it and then they would comment," said Betty.

"Then I had to do the General Store; we had everything. They got a peanut butter machine, I remember that. Ethel showed up with this electric peanut butter machine, and we made room for it at the end of the counter. Laws were so different then, but I had to make sure it was clean every night before I left. But it was fun, setting up and learning. I don't think she made any money on that; it was just like the coffee machine. The customers would order it just to see you do it. They would stand there and watch. Fred had a desk in the back room that I shared with him. But mostly he walked around pinching the duffs of women and making them mad. A friend came and worked for me, and she quit. Some people just laughed. I told him that some day he was going to get caught."

Betty continued, "I used to travel with Ethel quite a bit when Fred didn't want to go. I'll never forget the day we were going to an antiques show up in Philadelphia. We were riding up the pike, and we had to go around this circle and I can remember laughing at her. She said 'This isn't funny. How the hell do we get out of here?' That is exactly what she said. I said, 'Mrs. Noyes…' 'My name is Ethel,' she said. I would never call her Ethel.

"Every time I turned around they were paging me here or there. One day I remember almost falling down the stairs in that long dress, and Ethel yelled, 'Take that damn thing off! Go home and cut it off!' Here I am making these long dresses, and then I had to go and cut them all off. I think she was afraid I would sue her," Betty surmised.

"We would be there 'til ten o'clock at night. There were times I didn't get home 'til 1:00 a.m. They would let me go home to make my husband Bud's supper, one hour. How do you make supper in one hour? Fred would mind my hours. If I wasn't back in an hour, he would tell me about it. I would say, 'Take it off my pay, if that's how you feel about it!' I started at around forty cents an hour. Then Ethel said she was going to give me a commission on the stuff I sold. That lasted about three months; then she said I was making too much money.

"That's not all. The Noyeses would walk around in the evening. We would get notes in the morning. Do this, do that. Mostly it was if the shelves weren't full." Although Fred and Ethel hired good people and gave them lots of latitude, they never let an employee think that they, the "Possessors" of Smithville, didn't know everything that was going on.

"Back then everyone in Absecon went to work for Ethel," remembered Jane Betts Kubernus. "She had my mother up there working in the pantry! My mother thought it might be fun." The Inn had expanded from seating 42 in two rooms to seating 750 in nine dining rooms.

Work became ever more an obsession for Ethel, and she had little sympathy for those not willing to work as hard as she did. She had a consistent eye for detail and seemed to be everywhere.

She always came around to talk to each dinner guest, asking how they were enjoying their meal and conversing about family or business. One night, a patron was having dinner with her husband, a liquor storeowner, and his father, a fishing captain. Ethel came over to their table to chat. Nearby a young busboy was noisily replacing dishes in the hutch, an activity that drew Ethel's eye more than once from her conversation. She excused herself quietly from her guests and walked purposefully over to the unsuspecting busboy. Standing only inches from the offending employee, Ethel raised her index finger and shook it rapidly while her pursed lips moved quickly and silently. In less than a minute, she was back at the dinner table continuing her conversation. The abashed busboy had lost all his color and was working in a quiet stupor. The subdued hum of the dining room resumed.

At counterpoint, the playful and rambunctious side of Fred's character expanded. His station in the evening was at the entrance to the Great Bay Room with its magnificent floor-to-ceiling view of Lake Meone. Named after the bay the Mullica River emptied into, the large sunken dining room was a few steps down from the Galloway Room. Here, seated on a stool with his drink close at hand, Fred held court. Guests from New York, North Jersey and Philadelphia, as well as locals, chose to dine there so they could chat with their jocular host.

Chapter 7

CATAPULTING INTO THE SIXTIES

QUAIL HILL AND CREDITORS

She just wanted to do her own thing, and nothing was more important. There was no stopping her...She never knew how big it was going to be though.
—Bertha Lingelbach

U sing the language of the early days of inn keeping, Fred and Ethel called themselves "Possessors" of the Historic Smithville Inn. The company was incorporated under the laws of the State of New Jersey on March 28, 1960. On April 1, 1961, the Noyeses contributed all of the capital stock of three wholly owned operating corporations to the Historic Smithville Inn Holding Co., which held title to the company's principal real estate. Fred was named the president and chief executive officer and Ethel the executive vice-president and chief operation officer—pretty fancy titles for a former dishwasher and hostess. Fred was at the top of the company letterhead, although anyone who knew the pair knew Ethel was at the forefront of the operation.

The cigar box Fred used for cash had long been obsolete, and they needed a business accountant. They came to know accountants George Keppel and Carl Fiore through Mae and Ezra Bell. While Fiore served overseas during World War II, Keppel worked for the Bells and continued to do so when they went into partnership with the Noyeses. When the Noyeses bought out the Bells, Keppel turned the Smithville account over to Fiore. Carl worked for Fred and Ethel for more than forty years.

Fiore noted, "Fred was a nice guy, but he was basically a hindrance. She did everything. She was the brain, she did the work. She was very smart.

I think it was an era when people didn't have much respect for women in business. Ethel was smart enough to call him the headman. Financially, he was a nothing; she ran that place. Fred loved to hunt and fish and paint. I don't think he went to most of the business meetings. He was like a glorified host. They balanced each other; she was too serious, and he was too funny."

When asked about Ethel's business acumen, her ability to finesse a two-room restaurant into a dining complex and several retail stores in just a few years, Carl said, "Acumen is probably not a correct definition. Ethel had some strange ideas. Her idea was to buy what she needed but not to pay for it. She was always four or five months in arrears to her suppliers. She used these creditors as a temporary bank."

The accountants and the creditors weren't happy, but if the Noyeses had been ruled by the bottom line, there would have been no Smithville. Consumers had money in their pockets, and historic buildings were disappearing from the landscape. Opportunity was ripe. Neither timidity nor prudence held Ethel back.

As for Fred, he had more ideas than Carl realized. It was Fred's philosophy to use other people's money to grow a business, not one's own hard-earned dollar. Fred encouraged Ethel to borrow money when she wanted to expand.

Elwood F. Kirkman, a prominent lawyer, businessman and real estate tycoon in the area, was the president of Boardwalk National Bank. Born in Philadelphia, his family moved to Atlantic City when he was one year old. He attended local schools and graduated from Georgetown Law School in 1925 at the age of twenty-one. Two years later, he became a director and counsel for the National Bank of Ocean City. The precocious and formidable Mr. Kirkman was appointed a director of the Boardwalk National Bank of Atlantic City and became its counsel in 1932.

The Boardwalk National Bank was the only financial institution in Atlantic City to function during the Great Depression without consolidating with other banks or receiving government aid. The bank grew rapidly, advancing from deposits of several million dollars to $50 million in 1950. It developed a reputation for being progressive and was the place to go for a business loan. Fred and Ethel approached the bank for $500,000. Elwood Kirkman and his board of directors granted the loan with the contingency that Kirkman be on the board of directors of the Historic Smithville Inn.

Ethel knew she could not treat a loan from the bank the same way she treated an unpaid vendor or contractor bill. The bank loan was paid consistently and on time.

Elwood called everyone "Champ" simply because he knew so many people and often couldn't remember their names. He became Ethel's mentor. "Yeah, Ethel was good at getting free advice from everybody. She felt she was doing something good for South Jersey, and everybody should help her, that they should want to," observed Carl Fiore. "Kirkman took an interest in Ethel at first, but later he tried to take her over. I don't know if he was jealous of her or what. He did not like her success, so he would not loan her any more money. She always needed money because she was always expanding.

"Ethel had some odd ideas about financing," said Carl. "For instance, when I took over the accounting, she had thirty-eight bank accounts, one for every little store. She also had a holding company. It was the damnedest thing. We would have to go up there to reconcile the cash once a month. She didn't trust her bookkeepers to reconcile the cash. The accountants had to come in once a month and reconcile thirty-eight accounts."

Smithville took on a life of its own. Nothing stayed the same as more construction, more employees, more promotions and more customers created a whirlwind of activity. Fred and Ethel had outgrown their offices upstairs in the old Inn, and they planned larger accommodations in keeping with the style of their growing business. The new building was a colonial design, complete with a spire. But the demand for more dining space and the opportunity for more income changed the course of construction. The building was turned into a restaurant before it was finished. For their offices, the Noyeses bought the Gross house on the corner of New York Road (Route 9) and Moss Mill Road and decorated it with art and antiques.

The new Lantern Light Inn restaurant featured gourmet dining with full course candlelight dinners, unlike the more simple Early American food served in the Inn. The gracious dining took place in Patriots Hall on the second floor. The room featured a mural of the Battle of Chestnut Neck and was considered the loveliest of all the rooms in Smithville. "Beef and Beer" fare was served on the first floor in the cozy setting of the Spread Eagle and Golden Spur Taverns. The building was 7,900 square feet, housed four dining rooms and two bars and could accommodate 350 patrons. The Lantern Light Inn opened for business just before the holiday season, in November 1964.

The new restaurant needed a manager. The Noyeses traveled to the Greenbriar, a historic hotel and resort in White Sulfur Springs, West Virginia. "I think she was probably putting feelers out for people who had substantial background in the food and beverage business. Of course, the Greenbriar is the hub of the most professional training in this country," said Glenn

Kennedy, then director of food and beverage at the Greenbriar. Glenn was tall, handsome and smooth and carried himself well. Ethel was immediately taken by him. His background included working at the Castle Harbour Hotel in Bermuda and the Everglades Club in Palm Beach, Florida. He and Ethel shared the experience of growing up on a farm and quickly bonded. When Ethel learned Glenn's wife was from New Jersey, she said, "Why don't you come home to New Jersey?" Glenn was amazed by Ethel's direct approach.

In October 1964, the Noyeses sent pilot Wayne Kiser to fly Glenn to Smithville. He came up for a three-hour interview and was invited back for Christmas with his wife and three boys. The family stayed in the Noyeses' house on Sooy Lane in Absecon. The restored home was furnished with priceless antiques and decorated lavishly for the holiday, with presents under the tree for the children.

Glenn reminisced, "We went up to Smithville Inn for Christmas dinner. The carolers were singing outside in the softly falling snow. They drove the animals up in front of the Inn, the goats and sheep and donkeys and geese. It was an absolute paradise; totally different than anything I was used to. I was used to a very formal operation; stiff shirts, tuxedos and white gloves. It was relaxed, and I felt very comfortable with the Noyeses. They sat us in front of the fireplace, and she and Fred joined us. That's where it all began."

Glenn Kennedy went to work as the manager and maitre d' of the Lantern Light Inn. He found Fred "a very warm and cordial man. I think he always had a longing to have two or three little kids. She couldn't have any because right after their marriage she had an operation; he told me all about that. Fred and I became very good friends over the fourteen years I was there, and I enjoyed him. But Ethel was the leader; there was no question about it. She was the driving force." Glenn admired what she had achieved through self-motivation and self-learning, even though, she told Glenn, she just barely skipped by and graduated twelfth grade. She was a self-made lady who got involved in politics and became a good friend of Governor Hughes. They catered two or three functions at the State House in Trenton.

And Ethel liked Glenn even more because he was an earthy person. "I had the ability to go out and work the soil and the garden and plant and raise chickens and turkeys and stuff like that. I used to go over and visit her father, who lived in Port Republic. He only went to the second grade in school; I don't think he could read or write. She was always interested in the fact that I would go over and see him and really enjoy him."

Not everyone was happy, however. Fast-track expansion and irregular cash flow caused budget-trimming tactics that affected the income and therefore the attitude of some employees. "Smithville Pickets: Restaurant Workers Claim Poor Labor Conditions at Inn" was a headline in the *Press of Atlantic City* on December 10, 1966. "Appalling working conditions" were claimed by a group of employees. According to John Timperio, president of Local 508, the AFL-CIO Hotel, Motel, Club and Restaurant Employees Union, the complaints prompted a unionization drive and reportedly some 60 of the 120 employees at the Inn staged a picket and another 40 stayed out of work in protest. The Smithville Inn officials roundly refuted this report, saying fewer than 20 employees were involved in the picketing.

According to the article, the waitresses complained of paying for their knives to cut bread at the customers' tables. They were required to purchase the knives at the Smithville General Store for seventy-five cents each. The waitstaff also objected to having to purchase nine-dollar jackets and seventeen-dollar special waitress uniforms from the Inn, which could be bought elsewhere for less. Employees protested that timecards were pulled at the scheduled quitting time while they continued to work overtime without compensation.

The Smithville spokesman denied all charges. Godfrey P. Schmidt, the New York labor lawyer representing the restaurant, said professional unionizers were directing the demonstration. Ethel said, "There wasn't any way in the world that union representation could benefit our employees. We always paid beyond union scale; we always paid beyond minimum wage. Our employees want to work, but some have expressed fear of bodily harm."

Fred was not mentioned in the newspaper articles related to the strike, but he was very much involved. Al Black, friend of the Noyeses and owner of the Albert Black Detective Agency, was protecting the buildings and other employees from the strikers at the time. He remembered the situation well.

"There was picketing, and the union people were throwing nails in the driveway. A guy by the name of John was the head of the union.

"Well, when the nails went in the driveway, Fred said, 'This guy John must think he is dealing with a clam digger. I'm going to go out and straighten it out.'

"He took a baseball bat and chased John all the way down Route 9.

"Godfrey said there will be a suit filed with the Labor Relations Board, and Fred says, 'Well I hope he [Timperio] comes to court because he's not going to ruin my customer's tires or anything else.'

"Fred took charge when it came to stuff like that. A lot of people thought Fred did not have much to say, but Fred was the type of guy that let Ethel run everything until it came to a big problem. Then Fred would take action.

"Just like when they had the South Jersey Gas Company strike one time," Black went on. "Some of the picketers were going around and shutting off gas meters in a lot of places because it would take a long time to get the gas back on. The gas company would have to come and re-light all the pilots, and this and that. Fred Noyes said to me they had all their gas meters fenced in, and he heard they were going to shut them off one night.

"'Why don't you come out and sit with me?'

"I said, 'What's the matter, Fred?'

"And he said, 'Because if they decide to come, I want you to pass the word to the pickets and the gas company that I'm here and they are going to hear about the Noyes Law.'

"I said, 'The Noyes Law, what's the Noyes Law?'

"He said, 'If they go over there and shut my meters off, they'll be shot.'

"He sat there with a twelve-gauge shotgun waiting for them to come.

Ethel tried to stop him but he said, 'If they don't go past that No Trespassing sign there is no problem, but they try to shut my gas meters off, I don't care who it is. If they try to put me out of business and stop my economic right to make a living, I'll shoot 'em.'

"That was one of the few places that did not have their gas meters shut off in those days.

"Like I say," concluded Black, "Some of the big decisions wouldn't have happened if it wasn't for Fred. Not running the business day to day, but other things that Ethel would have tried to handle in a more diplomatic fashion. Fred, he would say, 'I was raised in Fish Town, Philadelphia and in Lower Bank and I can get down and play with the worst of you.'"

None of this slowed the forward momentum. "An airstrip that will be able to handle everything but jets will open in November at Smithville Inn," began a release in the *Press of Atlantic City* on October 28, 1967. The airstrip was a brilliant concept. It put Smithville on the map for aviators and their passengers, including business people, politicians and entertainers. Continuous auto shuttle service would be maintained between the field and the Smithville restaurants. The 2,200-foot-long and 60-foot-wide airfield would accommodate eighty planes. Initially, the field would handle daytime flights only, but plans were in the works for a lighting system for nighttime visitors, as well as a hangar and a lounge.

Clarence Hanselman, a pilot and former navy SEAL, was the contractor for the airstrip. His relationship with Fred and Ethel went back to when they first bought the Inn. Hanselman was nineteen years old and working for building contractor Henry Bonner. It was Clarence who unloaded the machinery and cleaned up the grounds around the Inn, which was falling apart and had no windows. He dug the first part of Lake Meone. Clarence remembered, "Ezra Bell was calling the shots, well, Ezra and Ethel. They were both very strong. Ethel did a lot.

"She befriended Kirkman and got some money from him. She worked with everybody else's money, and she was always behind. She was a creative person, and once she wanted to create something it was very difficult for her to stop. She would call me up on a weekend and say, 'You have got to come over' on a Saturday or Sunday night. She liked to pick people's brains, 'What do you think of this? Let's work on that.' She always had ideas and plans. I remember pricing the golf course they were going to build at one point. She liked doing what she did; it was her life."

Clarence's wife, Joan, saw Ethel from another point of view: "We used to go there for dinner all the time, and she would be there twenty-four hours a day at the Inn. As soon as she saw Clarence, she would come over to our table, and right in the middle of dinner, she would take him two tables over and leave me to finish my dinner by myself, while his was getting cold. You know, once I was right there, and Clarence was talking about how he was going to the Bahamas and she said, 'Clarence, are you going to take your wife with you?' I'm sitting right there! I might as well have been invisible!"

"She didn't like women," Clarence retorted. "Ethel knew how to work people, she could wine and dine the politicians and get whatever she wanted. I heard she never paid overtime. When employees called the Department of Industry in Trenton to complain, no one ever came down. If they had, she would wine and dine them, and that would be it. She was shrewd."

But it was their financial dealings that most affected the Hanselmans' opinion of Ethel, and they were not alone. The Hanselmans remember Fred Galligani, another contractor who worked at Smithville. "Ethel hadn't paid him, so he went to see her," said Joan. "The lobby outside her office was full. He was a big loud Italian guy, and he raised his voice up and let her know, 'You had damn well better pay me now. I'm not leaving until you pay me.' She paid him." Most creditors didn't have his chutzpah. They had to wait six months and more to get paid.

The person responsible for putting off the creditors was Irma Offner. The Noyeses had known Irma since she was a little girl when they bought eggs from her mother and father on Moss Mill Road. Irma grew into a pretty, bright young woman and went to work for the Noyeses. As it turned out, she had a talent for handling creditors and shielding Ethel from their wrath. She and Ethel became close. Irma was the only woman featured in the 1973 annual report. Her title was "Assistant Secretary," and she was photographed seated with the corporation executives.

Joan Hanselman recalled, "Ethel owed us $15,000 at one stage. She said she would pay us $1,000 a month. Well, she paid the first month, and the second. Then nothing for the third or fourth month. I kept calling. I never got to speak to her, but I spoke to Irma. Well, six months later and still no money, and we needed that money. So I got a collection agency and he called her every fifteen minutes for twenty-four hours. Then he said, give her a few weeks, and if there isn't any money, we'll send a big thug collector over to the house in the middle of the night to bang on her door. Well, he must have done it, because about a month later she paid in full."

Even with the difficulties they had, Clarence admired Fred and Ethel. Clarence came around in the winter when there were skating parties on Lake Meone with hot chocolate and cookies. One year, he dressed as Santa Claus and arrived in a helicopter with gifts for the children of employees.

"Not many people could have done what Ethel did. She was tough; a cold and calculating woman. Some of us always said she acted like a man, and she worked like a man. I couldn't say I disliked Fred and Ethel. Hell, you can't help but like Fred. She was very coarse to him in front of other people. Of course, he provoked her; he did gross things on purpose to get her attention. He was no dummy. He didn't care if she took the lead though. I don't think Ethel got the enjoyment out of what she did that she could have. She was too involved in the next project to stop to enjoy what she was doing."

Six days after the press release about the new airstrip, the dedication ceremony took place on November 2, 1967. The largest facility of its kind in the state, the airstrip was cited as a tremendous benefit to Galloway Township and one more milestone for Smithville Inn. The state commissioner of transportation was there to sign and present the operating license. Other attendees of note were Raymond Wood, the president of the Southern New Jersey Development Council; Richard Jackson, the mayor of Atlantic City; Sam Carvelli, the Galloway Township mayor; and "other well-known people in civic, political and aeronautical circles." The master of ceremonies was Jack Lamping, director of public relations for Ocean County, trusted friend, confidant and business associate of the Noyeses. A number of people flew to the ceremony, including Clarence Hanselman of Port Republic, who arrived by helicopter.

A year and a half later, Smithville hosted an air show that featured the Burlington County Sky Diving Club jumping from 7,200 feet with a thirty-second delay before opening their chutes. The Atlantic City Sky Blazers demonstrated giant radio-controlled model airplanes that performed aerobatics with the skill of piloted planes. Charging only two dollars per carload, the show was promoted as a family event.

The airport opened other opportunities for those with imagination and the entrepreneurial spirit. John Lewis was one. There was little live entertainment in the area. Lewis envisioned celebrities flying to Smithville during the summer when the Jersey Shore was its busiest. Stars would perform in a tent theater, which was simple to erect and easy on the pocketbook. Lewis approached the Noyeses about his dream. He said the crowds would come to see top-name entertainers and spend money in the Smithville stores and restaurants. Fred and Ethel leased ground to Lewis near the airport and the excitement began. The Tent Theater was in the round and could accommodate hundreds of people. John Lewis put up his own money and made all the arrangements. He got performers such as Liberace, Mickey Rooney, Ethel Merman, Zero Mostel, Victor Borge, Jimmie Durante and Ben Vereen. Smithville employees, as well as locals and visitors, loved it. They had the opportunity to rub shoulders with the rich and the famous, to serve a drink to Mickey Rooney or dinner to Ethel Merman.

Wilbur Hoch played the piano at Smithville in those days. "Mrs. Noyes was constantly asking me to do this or that. I had an agreement that at any time of the day or night, if I was not at work, I would get up in my tux and play. Well she called me. I was out cutting the lawn, and she said, 'Bill, these people just flew in, and they want some entertainment with their dinner. It's just six people. You won't regret it.'

"I didn't. There was a man that would give me twenty dollars every time that I sang 'I'll Never Smile Again.' That was a lot of money in those days. He did nothing but cry when I played it.

"My wife, Frieda, worked in the sales office there briefly. She took all the clippings from the newspaper for Mrs. Noyes about parties and conventions in the area. Ethel wrote letters to them saying, 'Why don't you have your next affair at Smithville?'

"Then Ethel allowed the theater in the round to be established," Bill said. "I worked every weekend the theater was open that first year. We had cast parties at Quail Hill, and I met a lot of stars. I sang to Cyd Charisse. Mrs. Noyes then took me over and introduced her to me. I was nuts about her.

"When Liberace brought his show to the theater, Ethel said, 'Bill, can't you write a song to welcome him to Smithville?'

"She thought that I could do it that quickly. So there was a young man in my office, and what do you think. We got together over lunch and wrote a song.

"Later Liberace said that the only thing that he remembered about Smithville was the goddamn bugs. He drew more people than any star that they had."

Unfortunately, the only show Lewis made money on was the Liberace show: about $10,000 for the week. Hot, humid nights; rain; and hordes of voracious mosquitoes discouraged the audiences. After one and a half seasons—eight weeks the first summer and only four weeks the next year—Lewis had to close down. In spite of its short life, many locals still have fond memories of the glamorous Tent Theater. (John Lewis went bankrupt, and Ethel purchased the theater—probably at a good price—in 1970. The Noyeses hired John Lewis to work at bookkeeping and auditing. The job included things as diverse as being asked to do counts of potatoes.)

It was the Quail Hill project that superseded everything else. The renovation and expansion of the Quail Hill Restaurant was simultaneously the source of wide acclaim and the beginning of serious financial ills. Ethel's sister Lois Muller believed, "It was the beginning of the end."

In his *History of the Smithville Inn*, Fred wrote about the Green Top Restaurant across the road that was run by a "very nice" German couple. The Noyeses purchased it in 1962 and renamed it Quail Hill after local Native American legend. The restaurant consisted of two rooms seating about 112 people and was used primarily for business meetings, private parties and conventioneers.

By the mid-'60s, the demand for space outgrew the modest restaurant. In an unbelievably short period of time, Quail Hill was completely renovated with a totally different theme and expanded to many times its original size. The massive complex more than doubled the space at the Inn, providing twenty-nine thousand square feet for restaurant and cocktail areas, and thirteen thousand square feet for service and storage. It opened to the public in April 1967. Author William McMahon wrote, "The new and exciting Quail Hill, with three dining rooms, large banquet room, spacious tavern and cocktail lounges accommodates more than 650 and is unlike anything in the nation."

Dining at Quail Hill was like dining in a fascinating museum. The atmosphere was "Down Jersey," recalling the days when shipbuilding was a local industry along with farming. There was a priceless collection of clipper ship models, whaling equipment, ships' carpenters' tools, farming implements, ships' wheels, rare primitive art and a fine collection of decoys.

One of the most colorful rooms was the Ship's Hold Tavern in the below ground level. It was fitted out so authentically that one could almost feel the roll of the sea beneath the timbers. The room featured huge columnar supports, heavy rustic beams, portholes and chandeliers designed like ships' steering wheels with hurricane lamps. Along one side was a massive mahogany bar that set the scene for rum-swilling sailors. Round spool tables with captain's chairs completed the scene. The tavern accommodated three hundred.

At street level, the entrance foyer was dominated by an enormous open-hearth fireplace, complete with old-time cooking implements. The grand banquet room, Powhatan Hall, was named after the disastrous 1854 wreck of the packet ship *Powhatan* on the Brigantine shoals. Other dining rooms were the Oyster Creek and the Wading River, featuring pine paneling from old church pews and fieldstone from the Great Egg Harbor River area. The Nacote Creek Tavern sported guns, decoys and paintings of waterfowl. Well-known artists and craftsmen were hired to add their touches to Quail Hill. The mural in the Wading River Room depicted life in Southern New Jersey, circa 1800. It was composed verbally by Fred and Ethel Noyes and painted by Shirley Tattersfield from the Philadelphia Design Company. Howard Bible, an artist from New England, made the signs.

Quail Hill stirred the imagination of its visitors. Brides-to-be wanted to have their weddings there. Children were enchanted with the labyrinth of halls and walks on the lower level, taking them past a mock cobbler shop, milliner shop and a blacksmith. There was a wooden covered bridge, the planks rising in a slight curve over imaginary water. A tollbooth next to the bridge displayed a notice that read: "$20 Fine for Driving Faster Than a Walk over this Bridge."

Masterminding this complex project while simultaneously managing the many restaurants and shops across the street was an impressive feat. But Ethel, the visionary mover and shaker, and Fred, the supportive behind-the-scenes decision-maker, did it.

Building and outfitting the magnificent restaurant was just the beginning. Even food preparation for the entire Smithville operation changed. For better cost and quality control, all food was received, weighed and inspected in the 8,800-square-foot commissary in Quail Hill. The food was prepared here, and every meal was sent by truck in closed stainless steel containers to each of the three restaurants. The number of employees expanded to over five hundred, including executives, administrators, supervisors, kitchen help, waitstaff, cooks and maintenance personnel. Opportunities opened for seasoned Smithville employees as well as newcomers.

Francis Xavier Burke, identified on his card as "Bo, the Friendly Bartender," was hired to work in the Baremore Tavern at the Inn in

1963. The house specialty was the Jersey Devil cocktail. "We used to sell millions of those. Applejack brandy, cranberry juice, lemon juice and Cointreau, triple sec, you know. Ethel would brainwash the waitresses by giving them ten cents for every one of those they sold, so if they sold twenty over the night, they would get two dollars commission. There was a good profit there. At one time, they actually gave away the claret wine. They poured a glass for everyone who sat down." When the new Quail Hill opened, Bo became head of beverage and was responsible for the bookkeeping, stocking the bar and staffing. He had as many as twelve bartenders reporting to him during banquets and events.

"When she built Quail Hill, which was a tremendous amount of capital for Ethel, I became bar manager," said Bo. "Quail Hill was a tremendous building. It had a wonderful prep kitchen downstairs, elevators and stuff. All the roasting pans would go up in the elevator. She would do 3,000 or 4,000 dinners on a Sunday, and the main Inn would do maybe 1,500. It was a grand place, you know, pulling up in your Cadillac under the canopy, someone opening your door."

This volume of business took a lot of coordination, but, Bo commented, "Ethel was very fortunate because she had her family doing some of those positions." She enticed her sister Lois and her talented husband, Bob Muller, back again from Venezuela. "She also had the Sheas. Her Uncle Bill Shea had worked in diners before she used him. He was about eighty-five when he finished up working for her."

Bo admired Ethel. "I would call her 'Herself' to my coworkers, she had such a strong character. 'Watch out, there's Herself.' She would dust the ship's wheels and the paintings and whatever she saw that needed to be done. She was there eighteen hours a day, earlier if the china and glass show was in town and the Noritake people were coming. We used to comment that the larger the business grew, the less we would see of her because she had so much ground to cover.

"Mrs. Noyes was a dynamic driver of people," said Bo. "Sometimes she would be verbally abusive. A waitress might be slouching against a cabinet and she would say, 'Get your ass off my hutch.' She broke it right down in common terms."

She also went through the trash with rubber gloves and retrieved items such as carefully wrapped steaks and unopened bottles of Crème de Cacao put there by employees who intended to take them home.

The building and expansion of Quail Hill went on into the early 1970s. To finance the work, the Noyeses got a second, smaller loan of $300,000 from Elwood Kirkman and the Boardwalk National Bank in 1968. Some bankers who came into the bar joked with Bo that they loaned Ethel money to get in trouble with. They expected her to get overextended and anticipated buying Smithville from her cheap.

Even in the winter, Ethel had a full staff and kept all the candles burning whether there were customers or not. She had a $5,000 unpaid candle bill.

Author and historian John Cunningham visited Smithville at this time. "I came to know Ethel and Fred quite well over a number of years," he recalled. "I was introduced to her on a bitterly cold December night when Wilson Myers, then director of public relations for the Atlantic City Electric Company, drove me over to the Inn.

"Ethel met us at the door, quite easy that night for there were few other customers. She said she would put us in a special room—with a roaring wood fire in the fireplace—so that we could imagine that we might have been sea captains from 150 years before, temporarily stranded in Smithville. Then she brought us hot buttered rum. Later, we went into a somewhat larger dining room to enjoy a succulent duck dinner."

Sometimes trickles of the financial strain reached down to the frontline employees. Stories circulated about truck drivers waiting to get paid before they would unload their shipments of food and other supplies.

Chapter 8

HOW IT WORKED AND
WHO MADE IT HAPPEN

S ixteen years earlier, it had been Fred and Viola in the kitchen and Ethel everywhere else. Ethel still managed to be everyplace, but the scene had changed. Promotions and features in the Philadelphia and New York newspapers brought hundreds of visitors daily to spend money in the twenty-five shops and dine in one of the several restaurants. Atlantic City conventions and trade shows, such as the china and glass show, bused their clientele to Smithville. The Atlantic City Racetrack, where Fred spent time and money, was courted for business too. Weddings and community functions were scheduled months in advance. On Easter and Mother's Day, people waited as long as four hours to be seated for dinner.

A carefully orchestrated system was set up to handle the crowds so that everyone, or almost everyone, went away satisfied. Dick Butler was part of that system. Dick had moved to South Jersey from New York City when he broke up with his wife in 1961. A few months later, he was in a bad automobile accident and ended up in a cast from his armpits to the bottom of his feet. He was laid up for a year and a half.

When he was ready to work part time, he went to Smithville, where he had friends. "I went to school at Pratt Institute in Brooklyn for architecture. I lived in a coldwater flat. Try living in a coldwater flat, having no heat, no stove and doing drafting. I was interested in renovating old buildings and that is why Ethel chose me."

Dick wore a metal brace and could not walk around because of his injuries, so he was stationed at the reservations desk in the lobby of the Inn.

"They had a switchboard for the whole operation that closed at five. Someone calling in before that time made a reservation with the girl at the switchboard. Before she went home, she rang down the reservations list. I would take over from there. Bert, Ethel's sister, had the hat and coat check concession and I was right next to her.

"I would be at one side of the reception room, and Ethel was at the seating control at the other end. Just listening to this woman was what got me. Someone would walk in, and what struck me was the friendliness of this woman. One of the funny things that happened was when Hughes was governor of New Jersey. He was a regular-sized man, but his wife was very heavy. In fact, Betty Hughes wrote a book on losing weight. She lost it then she gained it all back, God bless her. Ethel Noyes was sort of anorexic. When the governor and his wife came in the door of the reception area, Betty Hughes would look over and yell, 'Ethel!' And Ethel would yell, 'Betty!' And they would run into the middle of the room, and you wouldn't see Ethel; she was lost between Betty's breasts!"

Dick remembered Ethel as "a hard woman to work for. She knew what she wanted, and as long as you gave her your all, she was with you 100 percent. She was a taskmaster, but I learned more from her than I did from anybody in my whole life.

"She was a sharp manager," Dick went on. "She had her favorites, but her favorites were people she didn't have to keep after to do things her way; if she told them to do something, it would be done. I can't remember her firing anyone for anything besides coming in drunk, and even then she would give him or her a couple weeks off.

"Employees were looked after like family. If an employee was late and Ethel suspected he or she was at Jo Jo's Bar down the road, she would call and say, 'Are any of my employees in there? Because if they are, you get them up here.'

"She didn't want them coming in drunk. She was quick to reprimand, but she never yelled at anyone. Ethel knew how to get things across and you knew when she was mad."

"When I first went to work there," Dick mused, "and before the state clamped down on her, everybody that had dinner was given a glass of wine. The waiter would say, 'Compliments of Fred and Ethel Noyes.' It was a pink Chablis she got from Renault Winery. After we had finished work, the seaters and the hosts, as we were called, sat down in the end of the Baremore Tavern. We had a good dinner and coffee cups filled with this rose wine. Ethel never came up and said, 'Where did you get that wine; what are you doing with that?' She said, 'Oh, you always take cream in your coffee,' and she would pour milk in it. You knew you were going to have to gulp it down to get rid of it."

"The main thing was she treated us well. If she hadn't, the union would have been there a long time before. There was great camaraderie, we were a family, we worked together, we played together, we drank together. Without this, the best system in the world will not work."

When it was really busy, Dick was stationed outside in a booth taking names; everyone had to register with Dick. He used an electrowriter to write the name and number of the party and the time they registered. Then he punched the card in the time clock. As he wrote in the party, the information went to Ethel's desk in the lobby on the electrowriter, which held up to six names. If the guests were going into the tavern, Dick wrote that in too so Ethel would know where they were.

The room seater went up to the desk to inform Ethel when a table was available. Then Ethel called on the intercom to the reservation desk, and whoever was there went downstairs and paged the next parties. There was a loudspeaker in each shop and on the grounds, so if visitors were shopping or feeding ducks, they knew it was time to get to the Inn. Once in the reception room, they waited about a half-hour until they were paged into the dining room. The first page was an external page, and the next was an internal page. Mrs. Noyes had a person on the door who made sure no parties were allowed in the reception area until they were paged from outside. There was a host who knew where every piece of furniture came from, and he walked around the lobby and acted like a tour guide. Once a party's table was set up, Ethel announced, "We're ready for the Smith party of four, and thank you so much for waiting." People knew they were going to have to wait so they came early to get signed in. Some guests even went into Atlantic City if they were told the wait would be three to four hours.

"It was either Mother's Day or Easter, and near the end of the day," Dick said. "I had just closed up outside and had come in to get who was left. There was a customer, Mrs. So and So, who kept coming up to the podium, saying she had been waiting longer than anyone else, asking for special attention and generally being annoying. When it came time for Mrs. Noyes to announce the next table over the loud speaker she said, 'We're ready for the Pearson party of four. And will Mrs. So and So sit down and shut up!' That was the closest I ever saw Ethel come to losing her cool."

Dick added, "It's funny, all these things are coming back that I would never think of. If there was a very busy station in a dining room and a lot of people left all at once, I can remember Ethel leaving her place at the seating podium and going in and helping bus tables. Nothing was beneath that woman."

Nothing was beneath Fred either. In addition to being host and bartender, he still liked to go in the kitchen to dabble in the cooking and do some serious eating. Cindy Mason-Purdie remembered going to the Inn for the old-fashioned country breakfast with her father. "It was a lot of food, and my father liked the corn meal mush. Ethel would come say hello. Then Fred came out from the kitchen. My father laughed because Fred had flour and sugar all over him. When he saw Ethel, he ran back to the kitchen. Ethel always had him on a diet. Everything was just so, but Fred was in the kitchen eating powdered doughnuts. One time we saw Fred come out of the kitchen with a sandwich in each pocket."

Bob Muller, an engineer and a numbers man, was also part of the system that made things work. Lois said, "Bob kept records of everything, everything, all kinds of records. What the weather was, what the temperature was, what conventions were in Atlantic City. He predicted ahead for the next year. It was amazing how it all followed. The people showed up like cattle. He predicted we would have so many people such and such a night, so order this much duck. He usually came out within a meal or two of what was needed. He made sure everything was running smoothly in the kitchen. He predicted staffing, supplies, food costs, everything. We cut down on waste that way, and profits increased."

Even with predictions and supervision, things sometimes went wrong. Jim Paxson was a waiter at the Inn for twenty-five years. "I used to dash across the street to the Quail Hill commissary a lot to get things. We always used to run out of raisin bread, and I would run across to get that and hide the loaves. My parties would get everything they were supposed to have. A waiter would say we are out of raisin bread and I am sorry, and out I would come with raisin bread for my party.

"We used to serve flaming drinks, Foxfires we called them. It was Southern Comfort and crème de menthe. I can remember a number of them falling over; one went right on a lady's fur coat. We also used to serve Flaming Duck, duck with orange glaze. One night, a lady's hair caught on fire. I think they got in trouble for that. I wasn't there that night, but I heard about it. You should always put the lid on the bottle before you light the sauce, but they didn't and the flame jumped from the duck to the bottle."

Jim Paxson was proud of his long service at Smithville and proud of how the place was run. He went on to talk about what the restaurants offered customers. "One special thing we had was cinnamon ice cream for the apple pie. The cinnamon ice cream was made especially for the Inn. She also had cranberry sherbet specially made to put on top of the fruit cups. We served bay clams, clams casino, jumbo shrimp cocktail; we had the chicken pie. We had stuffed shrimps, stuffed lobster, whole Maine lobster. They had a tank in the lobby where you could pick your lobster."

Ed Davis, a radio personality at WFPG, remembered that Ethel believed in advertising and promotions. She had a year-round contract with the station. She didn't wait for the station to call her; she wanted to jump-start each season, so she called WFPG. Ed did remotes from Smithville. In the summer, there were promotions from the old-time ice cream stand. As Ed broadcast, free ice cream was handed out to children under twelve. At Thanksgiving, he rode on a stagecoach with a double team, wore a silk top hat and broadcast from the scene. Christmas was a commentary on the beautiful decorations, the door wreath contest and on-the-spot interviews in the lobby of the Inn. "Is this your first time? Why do you come back? Why do you like it?" There were many repeat customers.

Another employee who was part of the action-packed 1960s was Mae Carrow, a diminutive, energetic woman with a quick mind and sense of humor. Mae had lost both her parents close together in the late 1950s, and the doctor told her to get out and get her mind occupied. She went to the Smithville Inn, walked up on the porch and asked for Ethel Noyes. Ethel came out and chatted with her. Mae had office experience, but there wasn't really a position. When Mae left, Ethel said, "Thanks for coming. Maybe I'll call you sometime." When Mae got home, the phone rang, and "sometime" had come. Ethel asked if she could come out and give her a hand in the office.

"I got into public relations and marketing. I didn't have a college degree, but Ethel just pushed me into it." Several years later, Mae was running the marketing and public relations for the corporation with an office staff of five. During big promotions, the staff did twenty thousand pieces of direct mail, plus newspaper ads and press releases.

Mae liked the job because it was so diversified. "Even though my work was really advertising in the sixties, she might call my office and say, 'Mae, bring your crew over. We are short on service, and we want you to work the Port Republic Room.'

"So we would go over and man a room. She gave us the smallest, of course. None of us had any service background, and the people would love it. We just came in our office clothes, and the whole Port Republic Room would know that we were just a bunch of office people. They would tip us, and we would say, 'Oh no, please!'

"And then she would call me and say, 'Mae, we need some varnishing done. Can you come over and varnish?' That was in the Inn.

"Then one day we were going to have a wedding, and she had nobody to make canapés. So she said, and this was Saturday, 'Mae, can you come in? We need to make some canapés.'

"So she and I would go out in the kitchen, and we'd make the canapés. What I am actually trying to say is that when you worked for Ethel Noyes—not just me, this is everyone—you graduated; you graduated with top honors from the University of Hard Knocks. Get my point, what you didn't know, you would know before you left there. She would do anything. I never washed dishes. I supposed we would have if we had to. She just knew that she could dump you in a situation, and you would come out floating. I never worked holidays, but if push came to shove, I would.

"One particular Thanksgiving I did work. My husband came to pick me up, and I just told him off. I told him to go home without me, because I was so mad I was there so late. She was keeping me when she shouldn't have."

Mae concluded, "Ethel just liked it. Not the money, but the activity."

Ethel never took a vacation, or even a vacation day, unless it was business related. Trips to Peddlers Village or Old Sturbridge historic village were done with pen and paper in hand, as were meals in fine restaurants. There was even a notepad by her bed. Ethel often woke up during the night and jotted down ideas for the coming day. Sometimes Ethel woke Fred from a sound sleep to tell him to remember something. Fred just got mad. Activities that might be called hobbies, such as collecting antiques or trying new recipes, were all pursued to benefit Smithville, Incorporated.

Only Fred could interrupt Ethel's nonstop work cycle. He knew when to take her off the floor. When Fred said it was time to go in the afternoon, she went. Ideally they went home to Port Republic for a break. Or they might end up in the ShopRite grocery store and play around in there and buy stuff. That, to Ethel, was relaxation. It got her mind away from work.

One busy Mother's Day weekend in the late 1960s, a beleaguered gas station owner called Smithville. The call was forwarded to Mae Carrow in her public relations office. Cars coming in droves from Delaware and Philadelphia on Delilah Road were hitting the circle and stopping at the gas station to ask for directions to Smithville. The Hess station crew had enough, and they were not going to tell one more car how to get to the Smithville Inn.

"It was going to be a busy weekend, and we needed that business. So I went over to maintenance and told them to get a good sturdy post and make a sign with directions to Smithville. I got some people to help me, and I got the post in the ground and got my sign on it. Well, they served a warrant on me at home for trespassing. I had told Ethel that I may get away with it, but I might not get away with it if someone sees me. They may fine us for putting a sign on public property. Well I got the summons, and the fine was paid, but we got our money too. It was good business."

Good business indeed.

Chapter 9

THE ARTISTIC PURSUIT

The sixties were coming to a close, but it was just the beginning of new pursuits at Smithville. The first decoy show in southern New Jersey took place at the Quail Hill Inn in 1969. The well-publicized event took advantage of a growing interest in decoy carving and collecting. Top carvers of the day, such as Ernie Muehlmatt, Hurley Conklin, Gene Hendrickson, Armand Carney and Tom Carlock, were there.

The room was set up with many tables, each with a placard designating where the carver was to display his craft. Ethel arrived as the carvers were putting out their work. The number of decoy sales made that day depended, in part, on the way the birds were displayed, so each carver brought props to set off his birds. Grasses and branches and pieces of wood came out of boxes, along with a variety of shorebirds, meticulously carved and painted. There were ducks and hawks and shore runners and catbirds, but the birds that caught Ethel's eye that morning were two plumage birds. In Victorian times, when a lot of feathers were used for ornate hats, hunters shot plumage birds just for their feathers. Plumage birds were the tallest, most stately of the shorebirds, and many carvers never even attempted to execute their likeness. Ethel was riveted by the great heron, with its long neck and steely grey-blue feathers, and the egret, more delicate in size but striking with its snowy white plumage.

The birds were among a grouping put together by Gary Giberson, a local thirty-one-year-old who had been carving with his grandfather Alonzo since he was a young boy. Gary took to carving as other boys did to baseball. He worked at it and practiced it until he developed a style that spoke for him and the birds he studied. He bragged that he wasn't afraid to carve what others would not dare to try, birds in action and birds in flight.

No words were wasted as Ethel greeted the young weekend carver. "No, no, no. These are too beautiful to be stuck in a corner. I want them in the center window. Would you mind setting up over there?" And she picked up the name cards from the tables and switched them. Then she said, "How much is this? How much is that? Oh, I'm making you nervous. Price it all up, and I'll come back. I want to buy them all."

A native of Port Republic with a long family history in the Jersey Pines, Gary regarded Mrs. Noyes as if she were from another world. At that time, Port Republic, about five miles northwest of Smithville, had a population of about seven hundred. Most of the families there were residents of several generations. The Van Sants, the Cavileers, the Browns, the Bowens and the Gibersons all had roots in the past. They had been shipbuilders and seamen, clammers, tavern keepers and sawmill operators. The homes, except for a few, were modest old structures. If there was wealth, it didn't show. The only time Gary had ever seen Ethel she was in her Cadillac, sometimes chauffeured, riding from her stately home on the Mill Pond in Port Republic to her Smithville empire a few miles away.

He could hardly believe what had just happened. Within a few minutes, he sold everything, and the show hadn't even opened. Up to now, he had little luck selling decoys because hunters were buying cheaper cork, plastic and Styrofoam ones.

This was his first show, and he wanted to keep one carving, so he asked, "Mrs. Noyes, can I keep just this one?" Ethel replied, "I had my eye on that one; you have good taste. But you keep it. I have all the rest." And so it was that Gary Giberson was "discovered" first by Ethel and then Fred Noyes.

Except for the one piece, Ethel bought everything Gary had that day for $300. But she saw more in him than a talented local carver. She saw someone who would be an asset to the recreated South Jersey village she envisioned at Smithville. It was to be a living history showplace, like Williamsburg and Old Sturbridge Village. Gary loved to talk and tell stories, especially those he had learned from his grandfather Alonzo. Like Ethel, Gary was intrigued by the romance of the old days. As a boy, he used to go on the truck with his grandfather to deliver lumber to nearby boat yards. While sitting on the back of the truck and eating lunch from a brown paper bag, he'd ask the boat builders "a million questions" about steam bending ribs and how to use axes and hand tools, all of which helped him later on.

When Ethel came to Gary's table later that fateful day, she said, "I'm amazed at the way you tell stories about your grandfather, about duck hunting, the cedar sawmill, the cedar swamps and the Mullica. We're going to have a buffet dinner for all the carvers, and I want you to sit with Fred and me."

David Rhodes was another local carver at the show. Rhodes said, "Ovid Risso, then director of public relations, approached me as to what I thought about setting up the first show, about overseeing what benefits the carvers would get. I talked him into offering a dinner to every carver who was there, which was fairly expensive. Otherwise, at most shows you paid a fee and meals were on yourself. The Smithville show was unique. It was like a party."

Gary was nervous because he considered Ethel to be society. He worried, "How do I get an olive pit out of my mouth? I was really nervous because there was chicken. So I waited and watched her cut her chicken from the bone and leave the bone. It wasn't a barbecue where you pick up chicken with your fingers."

Gary's table manners were the last thing on Ethel's mind. She asked him where he worked. When he answered, "The Atlantic City Electric Company," Ethel looked right at him and said, "It's going to be really hard for me to get you away from them, isn't it?" Without pausing, she continued, "Can you come down and talk to me tomorrow morning?" She asked Gary what department he worked for and then said, "You're excused from that. Just come over at eight o'clock." She went on to say she had gone to school with Gary's mother and that she liked Gary.

Gary was duly impressed by Ethel's attention, but he had his own agenda. He was a lineman at the electric company and loved the element of danger. After 12½ years, he had seniority and good benefits and was on the management track. Recently divorced, Gary drove a Corvette convertible and was enjoying his newfound freedom.

Ethel asked Gary how fast he carved and was impressed that he could make three decoys a day. She got out her notepad and a pencil and showed him how much he could make working for Smithville instead of the electric company. She added, "I have three barns full of antique tools. I want you to go over there and pick out anything you want or need."

The next morning, Gary was sitting in Ethel's office discussing his future. She said, "I'm going to introduce you to multimillionaires, to governors, to show business people. You'll be making carvings for all these people. Let me tell you something, I'm in the restaurant business. Would you rather have a hot dog stand on the boardwalk or serve filet mignon to the governor?" Gary said, "Wow, Mrs. Noyes, you make your point well."

When he went to work that day, his supervisor said the president of the electric company had gotten a call from Ethel Noyes saying that Gary would be late for work and to excuse him. There was a car waiting to take him out to his crew.

"Right off the bat I'm thinking, who is this woman, who is this power? How can she do this? She just changed my life. And she did it in twenty-four hours."

Gary started working at Smithville just on weekends. Because he was part of the electrical emergency maintenance team, a telephone was installed in his carver's shop. If he was called in for an emergency repair, he notified Smithville security, and they closed the shop for him.

The shop was set up so Gary could do demonstration carvings and talk about the old days in South Jersey. He talked about how the art of decoy carving was learned from the American Indians. He used a Victorian-style carving bench called a schnizelbunk. He started with a rough-hewed block of Atlantic white cedar that was the approximate size and shape of the bird he planned to carve. His tools were a twenty-four-inch band saw, a drawknife, a wood rasp, a spoke shaver and a Stanley 199 utility knife. The final form was sanded down with three grades of sandpaper and finished with latex paint. His style was realistic, including carved feathers and other details, as opposed to the primitive style of some carvers. The mallard duck was one of his favorites because the male was so colorful and the female a challenge to paint because every feather had multiple colors in it. Each duck had its own personality: the canvasback was regal, the wood duck proud and the merganser racy. Gary sought to catch their characteristic movements, and some of his most exciting work was birds in flight.

He carved and talked, often nonstop for an hour or two at a time. "My grandfather Alonzo told me that God put the Giberson family on the Mullica River because it was the greatest place in the world to live. They were totally self-sufficient, living off rockfish, venison, rabbit, chicken, duck and small vegetable gardens." He also told people about New Jersey decoys, which were distinct in that they were made in three pieces. The decoys were hollowed out so they would float and ride high in the water with a lifelike movement. He talked about local decoy makers Jack Updike and Gene Hendrickson who influenced his carving.

The fame and fortune that Ethel promised Gary came true. The first person he made a custom carving for was Ethel Merman, a houseguest of the Noyeses while she performed at the summer Tent Theater. Carvings ordered by Zero Mostel, Victor Borge, Jack Carter and Ben Vereen followed.

They took their woodcarvings back to Broadway and Hollywood and showed them to their friends. Soon Gary was sending orders all over the country, plus trying to keep the store stocked. He was making about $1,200 in two days on the weekend, three times more than the $400 he made in five days at the electric company. A year later, he resigned from the electric company.

Gary remembered, "I was interviewed all the time, and they took pictures of me. I'm talking to people, just meeting all these people. When Fred and Ethel had somebody really interesting coming, she would say, 'Gary, I want to buy a woodcarving to give the governor or some celebrity. Make sure it's signed.'

"One day, I'm sitting there carving, and Governor Brendan Byrne flew in and I didn't know who he was. He landed in his helicopter in back of the Inn. All the geese all flew up, and one of the geese flew into the electric line and knocked out the power in the Inn. I came out all yelling and mad. Luckily, Ethel knew what was going on.

"I was South Jersey," said Gary, "and they wanted the world to know South Jersey. So they used me, they used my talents; they used my Grandpop's stories. They used my openness, my willingness to talk to people. Ethel loved me, but she also loved my grandfather."

Fred appreciated Gary's work, too. In the late 1940s, while Ethel was hunting down Dresden china and Chippendale furniture, Fred was buying decoys, ten and twenty at a time. Back then, there were only about ten men in America interested in bird decoys. It was not until the 1960s that decoy collecting became popular. Although Fred had started collecting first, Gary had the edge because of his longtime acquaintance with carving, wood and decoys. Fred's money and Gary's knowledge were a good fit. Together they set out to assemble the largest and best decoy collection on the East Coast.

One of the people Fred got to know while collecting was John Cavileer, a Port Republic clammer. His father, grandfather and great-grandfather had all worked the water. "Once you start clamming, you can't stop," John said. "Fred only lived three doors from me when he moved down here, I think it was '58 or '60. I got to really know him because of decoys. I made about fifteen myself, just to hunt with. Now they use plastic. Then I started to collect. The Noyeses had a place on Main Street, the Amanda Blake Store, where they had decoys and other stuff. I took my decoys in one day when Fred was there. What I had were decoys I hunted with when I was a kid. I showed them to Fred to try to find out who built them. He was a big-time collector. He tried to buy most everything I had for forty dollars. Fred didn't know who had made mine; he wasn't really that knowledgeable about them."

Fred kept around $40,000 to $50,000 in his checkbook so he could buy what he wanted when he wanted it. One time Gary told a story of trying to get Fred to buy an extraordinary decoy. It was a turnstone, a shorebird with a curved-up bill used to flip stones and clamshells to find the little bugs underneath. The seller wanted $300. The turnstone had flat sides on it, and Fred said, "That's a flattie, I don't want it." Gary explained that it was not a "flattie," but Fred wouldn't buy it. Gary ended up buying it with a loan from Fred. He researched the bird and discovered it was a Raleigh Horner shorebird, one of a kind, worth thousands of dollars.

"I'm very lucky," commented Gary. "I have a photographic memory. I never forget a painting, and I'll never forget anything artistic like that. It burns a hole in my brain. And if I see a decoy I can't identify, I'll say to myself, 'That's in so-and-so's book.' I use it like a reference. I'm very lucky to be able to do this."

Luck or not, Gary had started to develop his eye for decoys at age five, and with opportunities provided by the Noyeses, he expanded this skill for several decades.

Fred and Gary were also artists, and this was a second strong bond between them. When they became fully absorbed in their art, the creative process took over while the rest of the world rushed by. Their garrulous, Down Jersey personalities belied the seriousness with which they took their art. They wanted to learn, to be ever-keen observers and continue to be inventive in their respective art forms.

"If an artist's work doesn't change, the artist doesn't grow," said Gary. This statement spoke for both Fred's painting and Gary's carving.

Fred had an enclosed porch at the Port Republic house where he painted. At Smithville, he painted in his office while Ethel, Irma Offner and other office personnel went about their business. He propped his canvas, board, brown paper or whatever on his desk, laid out his supplies and drew, designed and played with color. When in meetings or socializing in one of the several Smithville restaurants, Fred doodled and sketched. One inspired work on the back of a menu portrays a bountiful buffet more vividly than any photograph could. Purple grapes, yellow pineapples and red apples are all outlined in black. The composition is exquisite, alive with bright colors and a variety of carefully juxtaposed shapes.

"Fred painted constantly," recalled Gary. "It was his joy in life to draw, compose and paint. He loved color. First the basics, red and blue and purple. Later, he got into a felt pen era and began to use more varied color combinations. Fred's father had programmed hole punch cards that set up the textile patterns for jacquard looms. Fred had a little box he really treasured. It was about the size of a Christmas card box, and in it were some of his father's designs. When you saw this box of cards, it looked like a very well-developed Fred Noyes painting, they were so unique. So I think his love of color and composition goes back to his father for making these paisley prints. I asked him, 'What did they make out of these?' He said they made silk neckties and fancy wall hangings.

"It was neat to look at art through Fred Noyes's eyes, hands and mind. It was really fun to talk about art with him. He taught me composition by using his hands, both palms with fingers pointed up, then moving his hands in relation to each other and asking, 'Which is more interesting, this and this? Or this and that?' His best painting was *Busy River*. Everything he ever taught me was in that painting. He said you always start in the upper left-hand corner, that is how you read and write. In the upper left are two geese flying, and their heads are pointed down across the line of the sailboat and your eye just goes right smack down to the lower right corner. There are two herons looking straight across the bottom at some ducks looking the other way, up into the picture. He dances your eye with motion all around this painting. I said, 'Fred, this is your masterpiece.' It's done on brown paper. When he got really sick, he said, 'I want you to have this. You have always loved this painting; it was one of my favorites too.'"

Their fascination with outdoor life in South Jersey affected the work of both artists. "Fred loved the phragmites, the meadow grasses, the cedar trees, the Mullica River, the mill pond in Port Republic. His painting really brought out a lot of his early days of fishing and muskrat trapping. He was a great man. I loved him with all my heart," said Gary.

Ethel consistently supported Fred's artistic pursuits. Together they collected early American folk art. And with Gary, Ethel shared her love for fine antique furniture. "Mrs. Noyes loved my admiration for wood. She had her bedroom all curly maple. She had a piecrust curly maple table and a four-poster bed. I would go up there and just touch the wood.

"She didn't really like the New York Antiques Show. She said they are a bunch of shysters, but she loved the Philadelphia Antiques Show. She had almost a private showing before it was open to anyone else. People would explain to her what this was and what that was. She'd ask me to look at the joinery and stuff. I could identify wood for her. I knew one was a cherry piece and one a Honduras mahogany or from the Philippines, stuff like that. She loved to buy really good furniture, old Hepplewhite, all the well-known names, all very expensive. She'd pay $30,000 to $40,000 for a piece of furniture. Ethel kept $125,000 in her checkbook; and this was not an interest-bearing account. This was the Noyeses' cash for their hobby, to buy things. No credit cards. It was neat to go shopping with them. She would buy Dresden china, and if there was a piece missing, she knew. She was well respected, what we call in the decoy world a heavy hitter."

Her artistic eye extended to the appreciation of good architecture. The Noyeses had purchased the handsome Odd Fellows Hall on Church Street around 1950 where Fred's mother, Louisa, lived for awhile in the rear apartment. (Louisa Bond Noyes died in 1959.) Next she and Fred bought the striking Daniel Tilton House on Sooy Lane, also in Absecon. The home dated from the mid-1800s and exemplified the clean and simple lines of the Federal style. The classic white clapboard structure featured black shutters that framed the tall, symmetrically placed windows. It was the perfect setting for their growing antiques collection. Unfortunately, it was well known there were paintings, furniture and other valuables in the house, and the place was robbed several times. So the Noyeses were ready to move when the historic Franklin Inn came on the market.

The Franklin Inn was located in Port Republic on a grassy knoll overlooking the Nacote Creek and the Mill Pond. The historic house dated to prerevolutionary days. It originally consisted of two buildings that were acquired by local author and historian Mrs. Harriet Sander. She joined the two buildings and restored them to a state of elegance.

John Cavileer remembered well when the Noyeses came to Port Republic. "Course, Fred only lived three doors from me when he moved down here, I think it was somewhere around '58. There was an auction over by the beach. They set up a huge tent and brought all the furniture out of the Franklin Inn and auctioned it. I think it went on all weekend there was so much furniture. Then they auctioned the house. Nobody could believe that anyone would pay that kind of money for a house at that time, $37,000 or something. Now it's just a drop in the bucket. I was right out front selling flowers, wild flowers. There were a lot of people there; of course I was little. It went on all weekend, and I sold all the flowers. I had no idea who the Noyeses were at that time. I started hearing about him in the '60s, when Smithville was being developed."

The house had gracious porches facing the pond and the creek and a multitude of rooms, each with its own story. It was perfect for Fred and Ethel. Next to the elegant dining room with a fireplace and wood-beamed ceilings was a cozy den with wood plank floors. Ethel and Fred each had a bedroom, plus a sitting room on the second floor. Fred could paint on the porch; Ethel could cook in the kitchen. There were herb gardens, expansive lawns and a carriage house. And it was just a few miles from Smithville.

More wall space meant more art. Ever since he was an art student in Philadelphia, Fred was familiar with the top galleries. The Newman Galleries at 1625 Walnut Street sold only the finest art, from old masters to contemporary painters. Andy Newman, fifth generation of Newmans in the art gallery business, recalls the Noyeses would come in at least once a month and purchase paintings for both their home and Smithville. "Fred was an exceptional man who appreciated all sorts of art. He was an avid collector, everything from primitive Haitian paintings to fine nineteenth-century works. He was not biased, and he had a good eye. He could pick out good art no matter what period or style it was."

Commenting on Fred's development as a painter, Andy stated, "He was influenced by all sorts of styles and periods. His early work was very Cezanne-esque. Then it became more abstract and cubist. Each period was influenced by a number of artists. After he built Smithville and his landing strip there, he was flying a lot. He flew to the Eastern Shore of Maryland, to Tangier Island in the Chesapeake or wherever; he flew places for lunch all the time. Flying influenced his work. Some of his paintings look like aerial images, where he had taken the patterns of the fields and the plantings."

The Newmans did more than appreciate Fred's art: they had one-man shows of his work. A newspaper article said, "While generally serious about his artistry, Noyes wryly advised a friend how to appear an authority on art. 'It's easy,' he said, 'Just step back three steps, stare at the painting and say, very interesting.'"

Andy Newman praised Fred for using his "genius" to inspire and support other South Jersey artists. One was Tony Rudisill. When Rudisill was a boy, he took painting lessons from Fred. Rudisill drifted away from art for awhile, but when he began painting South Jersey bay, woodland and wildlife scenes in earnest, Fred was there to help.

"Fred would buy a Rudisill painting every week or month to promote him and feed him, basically," recalled Newman. Fred introduced Rudisill and his work to the Newmans, and thus the artist began a successful career.

Fred guided Rudisill in his art, and they were friends. One time Rudisill was walking in Smithville with Fred. A woman recognized Fred and gave him hell for birds pooping on her car. Rudisill recalled, "Fred said, 'What do you want me to do? Put diapers on the birds?'"

Another artist who enjoyed Fred's support and friendship was Paul Stankard. Deemed "the greatest living master of the paperweight maker's art in the world," Stankard's long friendship with Fred evolved over ten to fifteen years. Fred, who was thirty-eight years older than Paul, encouraged the young man to be a source of inspiration, do beautiful art and be a resource for other artists. In turn, Fred was an inspiration for Paul. When driving on the Garden State Parkway in the dead of winter, Fred would point out the evergreens, cedar and holly trees and the view of the bay, the ocean and the wetlands. He loved the land so much he made Paul want to move there. Paul described Fred as gracious and charming, very likeable, but definitely not frivolous, as he was perceived by some. "His sensitivity was directed at acquiring beautiful things." Ultimately, Fred collected more than fifty of Stankard's paperweights.

In the midst of all the building, painting, collecting and managing employees, as well as nurturing and annoying each other, Fred and Ethel took the first steps toward establishing a legacy. In 1966, they started the Noyes Foundation to benefit young people. In its second year, the foundation awarded four $1,000 scholarships to graduating New Jersey high school seniors. As Mrs. Noyes put it, "We've long been stimulated by the conviction that not to read and appreciate history opens a person to the danger of repeating its mistakes and of neglecting its enduring lessons. My husband and I are very interested in seeing high school students learn from history. We know of no better monument to the people of this state than a foundation, which has this for its purpose. We want to keep history in front of the young."

They also attended to each other. Sometimes their caring was humorous, as when Ethel and Fred played games around his drinking and eating. Other times, the support was straightforward, as when Fred chauffeured Ethel to her ever-increasing meetings in the community or to her appointments with the hairdresser in Philadelphia. Not only did he drive her, but he also waited patiently in the car if she were detained. She watched over his health and welfare, and he watched over hers. "I'll tell you how the two of them meshed," reminisced Gary Giberson, "because Ethel couldn't work without Fred and Fred couldn't work without Ethel. If anyone asked Fred how it happened, Smithville, I mean, he would say 'She dreamt it, and I said go for it.' He was the support that she needed."

"Did I tell you what he would do with a peanut butter jar? He would go into the jar with a knife and cut the middle out so the peanut butter jar always looked full on the shelf. He knew Ethel wouldn't open the jar if she didn't see where it was cut down on the side. He would have the jar 90 percent empty when Ethel would find out. She didn't want him to have peanut butter. I said, 'Why does she buy peanut butter?' He said, 'Because I tell her to.' I just thought that was so cute."

Chapter 10

THE CRESCENDO

THE OLD VILLAGE

Her biggest desire was to develop the Old Village. She had good dreams, but she never had enough money.
—Carl Fiore

While Fred was collecting decoys, Ethel was collecting land. Her timing coincided perfectly with a surging interest in Colonial America. It started with John D. Rockefeller when he set up a foundation to start the Williamsburg restoration in 1926. By the 1970s, more than eighty colonial buildings were restored and fifty more major buildings were rebuilt on their original sites. Places like Sturbridge Village (1936) and Deerfield (1952) in Massachusetts and the Shelburne Museum (1947) in New York State followed suit and thrived.

Ethel needed land to create her working historic village. She and Fred easily applied their bargaining savvy to real estate. Shortly after opening the Inn, they began to attend local Galloway Township council, planning and zoning board meetings. Ethel learned firsthand what was going on and who was making it happen. In 1961, the township adopted a zoning code, referred to as the Master Plan, which designated all areas of Galloway Township for specific use, such as residential, agricultural, commercial, professional and various combinations of these. She made a point of getting to know the township officials and politicians and learn how the town plans would affect her business.

Helen Winkler was secretary to the tax collector, John Dermanoski, and was intimately acquainted with property in Galloway, as well as with land values and landowners. Ethel hired Helen away from the township and put her in charge of real estate at Smithville. John Dermanoski, however, had another version of this story. He claimed he and Fred were friends and often went to the racetrack together. Fred would question him about land values. He perceived Fred as the driving force of the couple, the man who called all the shots. One day John was having a quiet lunch at the Smithville Inn with Fred, and Ethel stopped by. She said, "I'm sorry I took Helen Winkler away from you." John replied, "You didn't take Helen away from me. I fired her!" A stunned Ethel had no reply.

It was Helen's job to find out what was going on in the township and report to Ethel. Accountant Charles Braun, part-time tax assessor from 1966 to 1974, remembered, "Ethel was very good. She would come with her pad and pencil to city hall. She had her information when she came, and she knew what she wanted to do. She came to these tax sales because she wanted to buy land if it was near her property. She got most of her property at tax sales. Ethel was a good businesswoman. The tax sales were published in the paper, and Helen probably watched that. Dermanoski would hold the tax sales in the afternoon, two or three o'clock. Ethel would come with Helen."

The Noyeses used whatever techniques were necessary to get the land they wanted at the price they wanted. Clarence Hanselman recalled, "She worked with Kirkman a lot; he was a wheeler-dealer. They ended up getting a lot of property in quitclaim. Helen Winkler worked on that stuff. They would go out and find these properties where the taxes hadn't been paid. You were supposed to advertise for any living relatives for a certain period of time. Well, you could advertise in Florida, you know, then just make out a deed and claim the land. They were involved with several thousand acres. There were times when they had these land sales, and if a stranger showed up, they would cancel the sale and reschedule it, because it was prearranged who would buy it. You could have bought all of Galloway Township for five dollars an acre. Nobody cared then. Nobody cared about these quitclaim things either. In all, they bought land very reasonably over the years. Fifty dollars an acre here, one hundred dollars an acre there. When the Noyeses finally sold Smithville, it was more like four thousand dollars an acre."

The Noyeses nurtured important relationships. Charles Braun said, "She invited all the township officials to Smithville. The League of Municipalities dinner meeting with the whole Atlantic County, the Freeholders and everybody would come there. I am sure they had to pay, but that is one of the things that Ethel used to push, 'Come down to my facility.'

"I had a Smithville credit card, and I also had a VIP card," Braun continued. "Show that red and white card, and that would get you in the restaurant any time you wanted. This is after I became tax assessor. It was one of the benefits she gave to the township officials at the time."

"Helen Winkler helped Ethel with the real estate there," Braun continued. "They would take me through the various properties. Sometimes the buildings would be falling down, and they weren't going to do anything with the property for six months or a year. I would say, okay, let's call it a partial assessment. You can't call that a vacant lot. So I would put two thousand dollars or some nominal figure on there, and they agreed to that. As they got restored, I would be in touch with Helen, and I would come put a figure on the value of that particular building. I would look at the building before and after it was restored. Helen was hired to 'worry' about the taxes, to see they were reasonable and to see they were paid."

As they assembled acreage, the Noyeses began to visit other historic sites in earnest. They liked to travel with Ethel's cousin and Aunt Daisy's son, Floyd Conover, and his wife, Marge. Floyd, like his father, was a painter by trade, and he was a good one. He mixed all his own paint, and he matched every drape and every wall color perfectly, even if Ethel changed her mind again and again. He met Ethel's impeccable standards and worked with her for many years.

Marge Conover said, "She always wanted to see what other people were doing, so we took road trips from Monday to Wednesday. She hadn't started the Old Village yet, but I think that was in the back of her mind. We went to Peddler's Village, and that gave her a lot of ideas, but that was up in the mountains. Then we went to Mystic Seaport to get the nautical side of things because that fit more with our area. She took bits and pieces from everything. She constantly carried a pad, and she took down manufacturers and prices of things. My husband always drove, and Fred would sit up front. Ethel and I sat in the back. So much was happening all at once. When you sit back, you think, how did we do all that?

"Ethel and Floyd were both perfectionists, so they bonded very well. Ethel trusted him. They were both early risers and liked the same things. One time in Mystic, there was a big fireplace, and they had the fire going and the coffeepot on before the people in the inn even were up. Fred and I came down a little later, and I said to her, 'How do you feel today?' She said, 'Oh, I'd give anything to sleep like you do.' She had a terrible time, you know, she would take something to go to sleep and take something to try to get awake. She was so wound up all the time. Now I understand that. They say when you go to sleep it isn't your body that needs to relax, it's your mind. She would have so much going on upstairs, she had a hard time going to sleep. Fred was laid back. He just went along. He was thrilled with everything that happened; he was thrilled with everything she did. He was proud of her; he wasn't a pusher though."

After their fact-finding visits to Old Sturbridge and Peddler's Village, Ethel decided that the entrance to her historic village would be separate from the existing Smithville. Visitors to the shops and restaurants at the Inn or Quail Hill entered from Route 9 (Old New York Road). To go to the Old Village, however, they would have to go to the Moss Mill Road entrance several hundred yards west. Lake Meone provided a natural barrier between the two areas. The lake also became the resting place for a graceful oyster boat, the *Thomas M. Freeman*. A visitor standing in the commercial part of Smithville could look across the water at the historic sailing vessel nestled at the wharf in the Old Village section.

The *Thomas M. Freeman* had been among a fleet of Chesapeake Bay bugeyes that dredged for oysters in the mid- to late 1800s. The Noyeses had seen a bugeye at Mystic Seaport, so when they learned of the *Thomas M. Freeman*, they were eager to acquire it. They had the boat sailed from the Chesapeake across the Delaware Bay, out into the Atlantic Ocean and then into Great Bay and up the Mullica River. The boat traveled up the Nacote Creek to Port Republic, where the ship's mast and rigging were taken down and fastened to the deck. The bugeye was hauled by a special trailer and launched in Lake Meone.

The popularity of the Colonial revival movement signaled the time was right for groundbreaking at the Old Village. The first building opened was the Pershing School. The one-room structure was moved from near Toms River, New Jersey, where children had attended school from 1871 to 1930. Under the guidance of Robert Haviland, superintendent of the Towne of Smithville, the schoolhouse was restored to its original state, complete with a potbellied stove, desks, chalkboard, recitation bench and the ever-present birch switch. There were no lights, and there was a water pump in the yard, which was boxed in during cold weather. Inside, a pail of water with a ladle rested on a bench, and each pupil had his own tin cup.

More than four hundred people attended the dedication on April 21, 1969, including leading New Jersey educators and civic leaders. Guest speaker Dr. Roger H. McDonough, president of the American Library Association, commended the Noyeses' valuable collection of seventy-six rare Jerseyana books installed in the school. The collection was donated to the Noyes Foundation as the basis for a Research Center for the study of New Jersey history.

The next day, Ethel wrote a thank-you letter to their good friend Jack Lamping, who had been the master of ceremonies and who had donated a history book. She enclosed a $250 Smithville gift certificate. Jack was a member of the New Jersey County Board of Chosen Freeholders in Trenton, and he had a public relations firm in Toms River.

More buildings were needed, and Ethel quickly identified a willing employee to help with the task. Steve Calvi was a nineteen-year-old college student when he went to work for Ethel as a waiter at Quail Hill in 1969. Ethel liked Steve's inquiring mind. She asked Steve if he would be interested in working on a special project. He quickly assented.

The project was to scour the New Jersey countryside looking for old buildings of historic interest and architectural integrity built during the Revolutionary War period through the early 1800s. Each structure must be aesthetically pleasing and authentic and serve a function, that is, show something about the way of life at that time. Ethel was associated with the Daughters of the American Revolution (DAR), which was a good source of information. She teamed Steve with her niece Chrissy Muller, Lois and Bob's eldest daughter. She sent them to Cape May County to scout out buildings suggested by the DAR or the Cape May Historical Society. Many of the structures were one-room cottages with no plumbing or insulation. They were the homes of whalers who went out to sea for months at a time when whaling was an important industry during the nineteenth century.

Ethel told Steve and Chrissy to take the Noyeses' chocolate brown Cadillac for their explorations. They crept around the old structures, took photographs inside and out and tried to determine if the building could be moved.

After Steve and Chrissy gave Ethel their report, she made up her mind. If the building was determined to be structurally sound, it was moved to Smithville intact on a flatbed truck. If the building was in delicate condition, it was dismembered with exact documentation as to what went where and then reconstructed in the Historic Village.

One structure that underwent the painstaking art of reconstruction was the 170-year-old gristmill discovered in Sharptown, New Jersey. The four-story building was in excellent condition, but it was large and complex. Hundreds of sketches and photographs had to be made before taking the mill apart and then moving it board by board to its site on Lake Meone. The only change was the installation of an electric motor to drive the large paddle wheel that was formerly moved by a flowing stream. Inside the mill, grain traveled by troughs and elevators to each floor to be processed. Corn was ground in the mill every day and cornmeal packaged and sold in the mill or at the General Store.

Superintendent Robert Haviland's crew at the Old Village project included twenty carpenters, electricians, maintenance people, specialty craftsmen and a full-time landscape architect. It was Ethel's joy to review construction plans and oversee the restoration work on a daily basis. With an eye geared to authenticity and perfection, she always had a suggestion. This was her dream becoming a board-and-mortar reality.

"Constantly, constantly, there were hammers banging," remembered waiter Jim Paxson. "Ethel wasn't happy with a lot of things. She would have them torn out and done over." Paxson added, "I was friendly with Mrs. Noyes, but I tried to stay out of her way. The best place was behind her—she didn't miss a thing."

Ethel aspired to Rockefeller's Williamsburg Restoration, and she was able to inspire others in this endeavor, but she did not have Rockefeller's deep pockets. Moving historic structures from all over New Jersey and then having them restored was just the beginning of the huge expense of creating the Old Village.

When Ethel decided they needed a board of directors for their burgeoning business, the first person she turned to was Joseph Kaufmann, an accountant from Egg Harbor City.

"I was a director out at Pacemaker Yacht Corporation," said Kaufmann. "Ethel told me she wanted to set up a board of directors at Smithville and asked me for recommendations. I wrote her a three- or four-page letter telling her maybe she should have an educator on the board, a marketing person, you know different people to get different thoughts, different ideas. It was from that she formed a working board of directors and asked me if I would serve on it, which I did."

Kaufmann knew Fred from prewar days when Fred came into the bank where Kaufmann was a teller. He knew Ethel from the Rations Board. Kaufmann found Ethel to be "very creative and very in charge." He said, "She was showing me around Quail Hill during construction. There was a display case, and a workman was putting in decoys. She looked at it and said, 'No, I want...' She told him exactly what to do. He was going to put in three or four; she wanted twenty-five."

The Noyeses assembled a diverse board of directors as recommended. Kaufmann said they had great meetings, and Ethel always made sure the bakery supplied them with something to eat.

"One of the most interesting things to me," continued the account, "was even though they did a great amount of business, they wound up making little or no profits, and their cash flows were very poor because she was continuously building. She had a carpenter, and he had four or five people under him who worked around the clock. Dollar-wise, it may not sound like a lot today, but I guess their payroll was drawing out $1,000 or $1,500 a week. At one of the monthly board meetings, we passed a motion to the fact that these people would be laid off and some of these projects would not be done because the funds just weren't available. Well, she did it, she laid them off, and I'm not sure if it was the next board meeting or the one after, but they were all hired back."

Ethel had a craftsman named Dana Bible from Connecticut who drew sketches of all the things she wanted to do. She brought the sketches to a board meeting to talk about priority, which projects should be done. One set of color sketches was of a carousel that was to be an ice cream place. This was not voted a priority, but, said Kaufmann, "Ethel went ahead and did what the hell she wanted. They owned the business 100 percent, so they had the final say." This left the board distressed about the cash outflow and increasing debt.

It was Fred who firmly believed that entrepreneurs use other people's money to make their own businesses grow. Kaufmann agreed, but the extent to which they used their vendors as a bank was unusual. "Even though they were cash poor, they continued to operate," observed Kaufmann. "They kept buying up this land she had ideas for. There was just no end to the things she wanted to do."

Not having enough money to fund employee positions was also an issue. A few years after Mae Carrow left to have more time with her two young daughters, Ethel asked Mae to come back as director of marketing and public relations. Mae met with Donald Atkins, vice-president of finance. He told Mae there was no budget for that position, and he recommended she not take it. And she didn't. Next Ethel offered to pay Mae under the table if she returned as "historian" for the Old Village. This she agreed to. Mae became Smithville's full-time historian in 1972.

"For the two years that Ethel paid me, what I did is go back through however many sources to find out who the original owner was and then to get the history of the building."

Mae was interviewed by reporter Frank Corrado for the *Press of Atlantic City* while walking through the restoration site on May 23, 1973.

Mae said her primary job was to authenticate a building before Smithville would accept it. "So many historical settings don't give you any idea of what it was to live there," she said. "There's no dust on the table, no embers in the fireplace. What I want to give this village is the 'dusty' feeling, the sense that the building's owner just stepped out and will be back in half an hour.

"The actual building restoration adheres to procedures set down by the state Historical Preservation Commission," stated Mae Carrow. "We use lumber dating from the period, or, if none is available, hand-cut lumber of the same type of wood."

The opening of the complete village of thirty-eight buildings was planned for the fall of 1974. "This is not a commercial development," said Mae. "We feel very strongly about that. We want this to be a typical village."

Once a building was restored, it needed to be outfitted. Ethel's sister Bert was entrusted with that job. Mae Carrow recalled, "Bert worked tooth and nail on that Old Village. I did the research on the Quaker Church, an 1830 meetinghouse brought from Woodstown, and Bert did the interior. Bert was as good as Ethel Noyes at envisioning what should go in there, and all she had was some research. Ethel couldn't pass up a good antique, so Bert had a lot of things to work with. She did a marvelous job."

Bert affirmed, "I worked from the very beginning in each one of these houses as they were finished. I cleaned them after the men finished working." Bert moved many pieces of furniture from storage, even into buildings where the steps had not been put on yet. After a while, she began to have a lot of trouble with her hips. But she did not complain.

For all she did, Bertha was not invited to the grand opening of the Old Village. Many dignitaries, including the governor, were there, but not Bert.

To bring alive the Old Village, artists and crafters were hired to dress in period costume and demonstrate spinning, weaving, candle making, doll making, carving, blacksmithing and pottery making.

Ethel transferred Dick Butler to the other side of Lake Meone to become a manager. One of Dick's jobs was to find employees for the Old Village.

"The spinster, Jane Brown, and I were friends, and somebody was after me to give Jane a job. I said 'Oh no, she's not the type.' But I happened to have the costumes at home, so I said, 'Jane, go in the bedroom and put on one of those costumes.' She did and came out, and I said, 'Oh my God, you're perfect.' Jane was hired to demonstrate candle making."

Dick fascinated visitors with his stories of the old days when he led tours through the Old Village. "The women wore their caps down on their heads to keep their hair from catching fire while cooking in the fireplace and to keep lice out. People didn't take baths in the winter so their hair became greasy, and they had terrible body odor. Women took to fainting, the smell was so bad. The men wore leather, and the smell would come through. They wore long nightshirts down to their knees, and then they would just put a pair of pants on over them during the day." Dick even wore one of these costumes himself.

As manager, he made the rounds from building to building to make sure everyone was doing his or her job. Ethel wrote guidelines for wearing full costume, no jewelry, little makeup and so on. There were explicit instructions for the care of the costumes, including proper cleaning and ironing. All costumes must be washed in cold water and Woolite, not hung in the sun to dry and no dryers or bleach could be used. Other handwritten instructions included spraying for insects and keeping animal droppings cleared away by "a man with a little wagon to keep grounds clean."

When the Old Village was closed during the winter because there was no heat, Dick spent the time doing research in the Noyeses' library. Then he traveled to the area schools to give slide shows and entertain the children with stories. He told of feeding the cattle marsh grass, also called salt hay, in the winter so they drank more water and fattened up and would bring more money in the marketplace. He talked about the Coopers Landing stagecoach and described how anyone at Smithville who wanted to get on would lower the big ball that hung outside the Inn. He related how the women slept upstairs at the Inn, and downstairs the men slept with their feet to the fireplace. Dick always had an answer for the schoolchildren's questions, and if he didn't, he made one up. These lectures promoted business at Smithville. When the weather became warm, the schools sponsored bus trips to the Old Village. Sometimes there were four or five buses a day.

Among the live cast of characters in the Old Village was the vociferous and unabashed carver Gary Giberson. "You know, I can say I am the best demonstrating craftsman in America. And the reason I can say this is I've been to Williamsburg, I've been to Sturbridge, I've been all over. I have never seen a craftsman who could captivate an audience and talk to them the way I do. I can talk for an hour and forty-five minutes, two hours, and people's eyes never leave me. If I see I'm losing my audience, I have an unbelievable way of shifting gears and going into a subject where I can keep their attention."

The Old Village was more than a stage for Gary. It was there he met his wife, Niki, an artist and a student at nearby Richard Stockton State College who was hired as a spinner and weaver.

"You know, I would have never met Niki if it wasn't for Smithville," recalled Gary. "Dick Butler hired her as a spinner and weaver. I saw her walking across the village green, and I said, 'Wow.' She was beautiful. I just fell in love with her the first time I ever saw her. I found out that she knew how to do cross weave and was a very good artist. So I caught her by coming in twenty minutes early and going over to her loom and dismantling it and putting in wedges so it wouldn't work. I unbalanced her loom. Then I was called to fix her loom. And that's how we started."

Niki added, "I didn't understand it. I wondered, is it the humidity in the room, the fireplace? I didn't understand it. Then Gary would come in and say, 'Oh, I can fix it.' We were all in costume, of course. We were called the Village cast; we were like actors in a play." And a romantic play at that.

Enter Sid Ascher, public relations wizard. It was blatantly evident that visitors alone would not support the investment and overhead in the Old Village. According to Sid, the Noyeses were considering taking Smithville public and sought an expert to polish the corporate image. Fred and Ethel were told they needed to get Sid Ascher, a star maker in New York City who had promoted Vic Dimone and Tony Bennett. He worked in a busy Manhattan office and handled about forty accounts. In late 1972, Ethel's secretary called and set an appointment for Sid to come down to meet with the Noyeses.

Sid was impressed with Fred and Ethel's operation and agreed to take over their advertising and promotions. He regarded Ethel as a visionary. "She could look at a piece of land and know how it would look when it was developed." He also thought Ethel had a dual personality. She had her professional side, but she could swear like a longshoreman. As for Fred, Sid saw him as a dreamer. Ethel appeared to be the boss, but in a quiet way, Fred got what he wanted.

The first target of Sid's publicity campaign was Ethel herself. Ethel always looked great, but she had a gap in her front teeth and did not like to be photographed. So Sid took candid shots. Ethel said she didn't know what Sid was up to, saying, "Oh, there's that Mr. Ascher again." When the Madison Avenue Stylist Guild contacted Sid to nominate someone not nationally known as a well-dressed businesswoman on a budget and do it in forty-eight hours, Sid had a plan. Although he knew Ethel spent $15,000 to $20,000 a year on clothes, he nominated her. In March 1973, the guild committee came to Smithville and gave Ethel an award as one of the ten best-dressed female executives. Ethel was asked what her secret was to dressing well with her busy schedule. "There is no secret. I enjoy clothes, and my husband is the greatest guy to shop with in the whole world. He has a marvelous sense of color and design. We have fun shopping together."

Betty Loveland wasn't quite as enthusiastic about Ethel's wardrobe. She was running the post office in Smithville at the time. "The Noyeses brought a post office there, and I was supposed to run that. I didn't know anything about running a post office. It was confusing because there was another Smithville in New Jersey. She wanted the post office to send all these gowns back. I would say, 'This is worn, Mrs. Noyes. I can't send this back.' She would say, 'You wrap it up, and send it back like I told you.'"

When Ethel told Sid she worried she didn't have a college degree, Sid told her she knew more than many college graduates. He called President Bjork of Richard Stockton State College. President Bjork met with Sid the following week, and soon Ethel was awarded an honorary degree.

Sid also took charge of promotions. He instituted bridal shows at Smithville, opening a whole new market of vendors and customers. He scheduled a show in January when there was little else going on and one in June, the month of weddings. Other promotional events were organized around holidays, including Valentine's Day dances.

St. Patrick's Day became a major happening. Sid called an Irish airline to bring in two slabs of Irish sod, and in return, he offered to hand out the airline's posters. The sod had to be steamed twenty-four hours before coming inside. Four pretty airline attendants in uniform were presented as the young ladies who flew the sod over. In spite of everything, the sod didn't look too good, and the gardener had to spray green paint on it. The well-publicized affair drew the Irish from all around. One woman called to ask if she could bring her ninety-year-old father over to step on the sod. When he did, the old man cried.

Sid barraged the *Press of Atlantic City* with articles that built to a crescendo: "Smithville Is Planning Museum Village Project," "Smithville 'Backs Up' To Success" and "Makes Old Houses New." Ethel's regal vision was crowned with Ascher's words. "Historians and educators agree that the Old Village is the most meaningful restoration in the East because it presents a time and a way of life as it was, and never will be again."

Smithville Inn before grand entrance addition, circa 1958–60. *Courtesy of Ed and Wendie Fitzgerald.*

Smithville Inn, the Leeds Room, one of the original small dining rooms, circa 1960. *Courtesy of Irene Hartman.*

Employees dancing at a five-year Employee Recognition party. *Left to right:* Edna Marshall and Toni Olivier Smith, 1960s. *Courtesy of Edna Marshall.*

Previous, top: Thanksgiving. Antoinette "Toni" Olivier Smith in the Red Room, one of the two original small dining rooms at the Inn. *Courtesy of Toni Olivier Smith.*

Previous, bottom: General Store, Village Shoppes, circa 1959. *Courtesy of Jim and Barbara Ingersoll.*

Waitress Toni Olivier Smith at a buffet in the Great Bay Room, mid-1960s. *Courtesy of Toni Olivier Smith.*

Previous, top: Ethel dancing and having fun! *Courtesy of Edna Marshall.*

Previous, bottom: Absegami Room, Smithville Inn, circa 1965. *From the collection of Allen "Boo" Pergament, an Atlantic City historian.*

Above, top: The Lantern Light Inn at Smithville, 1965. *Courtesy of Irene Hartman.*

Above, bottom, left to right: David Burrows, Glenn Kennedy, Wayne McCracken and Robert Merrill, 1973. *Courtesy of Carl Fiore.*

Opposite, top: Bob Muller and Lois Lingelbach Muller, Ethel's sister, 1960s. *Courtesy of Irene Hartman.*

Opposite, bottom: Elwood Kirkman (left), banker, lawyer and early mentor to Ethel, with Ethel and Fred, presenting the Distinguished Achievement Award on behalf of the Southern New Jersey Development Council, May 1972. *Courtesy of Tony and Fran Coppola.*

Quail Hill Inn at Smithville, circa 1970. *Courtesy of Ed and Wendie Fitzgerald.*

Quail Hill, circa 1968. *From the collection of Allen "Boo" Pergament, an Atlantic City historian.*

Above: The Franklin Inn on Mill Road in Port Republic was made into a "showplace of the vicinity" by Harriet S. Sander and is on the National Historic Register. The Noyeses bought it and lived here from 1965 to 1987. *Photo by Joe Courter.*

Right: Ethel at home at her desk in the living room of the Franklin Inn, Port Republic. *Courtesy of Niki and Gary Giberson.*

Above, top: The upstairs study where Fred and Ethel sometimes took respite in the late afternoon before going back to work at Smithville. *Courtesy of Joyce Schiereck.*

Above, bottom: Smithville Inn, circa 1970. *From the collection of Allen "Boo" Pergament, an Atlantic City historian.*

Left to right: William Richardson, Irma Offner and Sid Ascher, 1973. *Courtesy of Carl Fiore.*

Fred W. Noyes and Ethel Marie Noyes. *Courtesy of the Noyes Museum of Art.*

Toni Olivier by the Grist Mill, which was moved from Sharptown, New Jersey. *Courtesy of Toni Olivier Smith.*

Previous, top: The *Thomas M. Freeman*, a Chesapeake Bay oyster boat known as a bugeye, being hauled out of the Nacote Creek in Port Republic and loaded on a trailer to be moved to its resting place in Lake Meone at Smithville. The boat was sailed from the Chesapeake up the coast through the Atlantic City Inlet to Great Bay and from there up the Mullica River to the Nacote Creek tributary pictured here, circa 1964. *Courtesy of Ken Smith, the Chicken Coop.*

Previous, bottom: Fred at the 4H Fair, about 1968. The Noyeses bought prize animals to use for beef or to bring to Peaceable Farm, part of the Historic Towne of Smithville farthest to the west on Moss Mill Road. *Courtesy of Ken Smith, the Chicken Coop.*

Above: Cranberry sorter on the second floor of the Grist Mill. *From left to right:* Betty Hughes, Governor Hughes's wife; Ethel; Virginia Lamping; and Toni Olivier Smith, right front. *Courtesy of Toni Olivier Smith.*

Left: Dick Butler and Emily Brown in period costumes replicating 1812 in South Jersey. They stand at the entrance to the Old Village to welcome visitors, circa 1975. *Courtesy of Dick Butler.*

Candle maker
Jane Brown
making candles in
the Old Village.
Courtesy of Gary and
Niki Giberson.

Niki Giberson at
her spinning wheel
in the Old Village.
Courtesy of Gary and
Niki Giberson.

Patrick Sheehan, Smithville general manager; Ethel; and John E. Campbell, president of the Scenic and Wildlife Attractions division of the American Broadcasting Corporation. *Courtesy of the Noyes Museum of Art.*

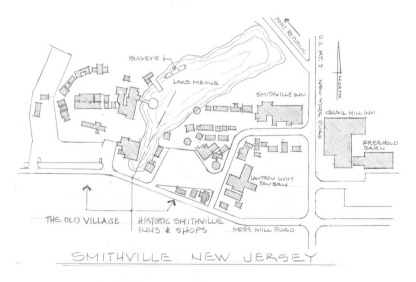

Site plan of Smithville delineating the Historic Inns and Shops to the east and the Old Village to the west. When ABC made a decision to build a bridge over the narrowest part of Lake Meone, the Noyseses resigned from managing Smithville. *Drawing courtesy of Joe Courter.*

Chapter 11

STORM CLOUDS GATHER

TROUBLE IN PARADISE

Leaders are visionaries with a poorly developed sense of fear and no concept of the odds against them.
—*Robert Jarvik, inventor of the Jarvik-7 artificial heart*

During the late 1960s and early 1970s, Fred and Ethel received awards and appointments at an astounding rate. In 1965, Fred served as chair of the Galloway Township Tercentenary Committee, and Ethel belonged to ten organizations. By 1975, the Noyeses' community leadership positions and awards numbered more than twenty-five and took a full page in William McMahon's third book about Smithville.

"You have to remember that it was more difficult in Ethel's day to achieve success as a woman," said author and historian John Cunningham. "In the 1950s, a woman's place was in the home. Did you know that if a woman worked for Prudential Insurance, she couldn't marry? If she did, she had to quit because she had a husband to support her. It was almost a giant welfare agency filled with spinsters and pseudo-spinsters. By pseudo, I mean people that were hiding the fact that they were married. In essence, they could not have children. I had friends that were married for thirty years and never told anyone. The *News* had female employees, but they all worked on the women's pages. Women were not as educated as they would become, so Ethel in some sense was a pioneer. Opening a tearoom is not pioneering, but turning that tearoom into a major business is."

The Women's Movement no doubt contributed to Ethel's recognition. She was sought after in the community and appointed to the Governor's Commission on the Status of Women. Her success as a female entrepreneur exemplified the "liberated woman."

Ethel had an interesting point of view on the subject, however. The *Press of Atlantic City* columnist Sonny Schwartz wrote on November 19, 1972, "The rising popularity—or unpopularity—of Women's Lib (Liberation) is never considered by Mrs. Noyes. 'I guess I'm so absorbed in achieving my own goals, I've never bothered to consider whether it's a man's world,' she laughed. 'I do know one thing, however. Many people might think of me as a woman executive…but I view myself as the wife of Fred Noyes.' This she said while munching a slice of freshly baked pumpkin pie."

Just a few months prior, on June 23, 1972, the *Press of Atlantic City* announced "Mrs. Noyes Elected to Industry Board," citing Ethel's appointment to the board of directors of South Jersey Industries, Inc., the area gas company. "Mrs. Noyes, the first woman to serve on the board, was elected after the board voted to increase its number from 10 to 11 members. Mrs. Noyes proven ability and energy has established her as one of the outstanding professional women of our state,' said William A. Gemmel, President." The remainder of the brief article was a list of Mrs. Noyes's other affiliations and organizational awards, fourteen in all.

To keep pace with the times, Gemmel and the other directors wanted a woman on the board. "I think that if we didn't bring Ethel on the board, the electric company would have gone after her. There was no lady you would want more than Ethel Noyes," stated Gemmel.

"I didn't think she would say yes. I went over around five o'clock with Elwood Kirkman, who had been on the board since 1949. He was a hard-nosed banker who did a lot for the area. You liked him or hated him. He pushed the envelope, broke laws and did unethical things. But he provided money through the bank for many things. We sat at a table in the main dining room at Quail Hill. We asked Ethel if she would consider it, being on the board. She asked a lot of questions. She said she was overwhelmed, and she needed to discuss it with Fred first. Fred said yes to Ethel, and Ethel said yes to us and we never regretted it.

"I had a lot of respect for Fred," added Gemmel. "He guided Ethel more than people think. I was amazed at his paintings.

"Ethel was one of the first ladies to be on a corporate board of a company listed on the stock exchange," continued Gemmel. "We met monthly. She didn't say very much for the first couple meetings; she just listened. That was important, because when she did talk, the board listened. She never rattled on. She made her mark. If she had something to say she would say it.

"I think Ethel thought, 'What is my purpose on this board? I will push for more qualified women to be promoted to more responsible positions.' It wasn't long after she got used to the men on the board that she would bring women's issues to the table. She let us know in a nice way that she thought women should play a more important role in corporate life than they presently did. It was the first time any of us had thought about getting ladies into management positions. As far as South Jersey Industries was concerned, she was the one who brought it up first, and we acted on it. I am inclined to think we would have done it eventually, but not as early as we did without Ethel," Gemmel concluded.

An avalanche of appointments and awards followed, notably the distinguished achievement award from the Southern New Jersey Development Council and Ethel's appointment to the board of governors of the Atlantic City Hospital in September 1972. Previously Ethel had served as associate chair of the hospital's gifts committee and raised $1.5 million for the expansion of the hospital. Accountant Joseph Kaufmann remembered, "The board of the Atlantic City Medical Center had an event called the Century Ball to raise money. When Ethel ran the ball, it was always more spectacular."

One of Ethel's favorite community initiatives was the founding of the Atlantic County Cultural and Heritage Commission. The State charged each county to form a commission to prepare for the 1976 Bicentennial Celebration of the 200th birthday of our country. The Atlantic County Board of Chosen Freeholders passed a resolution in 1971 to establish the commission to "promote public interest in local and county history, in the arts, and in the cultural values, goals and traditions of the community."

"Well, I am the original Atlantic County Cultural and Heritage Commission. I formed that with Ethel," said Florence Valore Miller, champion of the arts in the Atlantic City area. "We took to each other right away. She was a lady to the end of her fingertips. She taught me how to carry a big stick and speak softly. I would get so angry when something would happen, and she is the one who told me I would accomplish more if I were quiet. She taught me a lot, but then, I did a lot for her. She wanted more of a relationship with Atlantic City, but she didn't want to do it under her name. She met with me, and she asked me every question she could think of! When I went to my meetings, she would tell me things that she wanted to know. She liked to know the atmosphere and tempo of the city, how did that feel. A lot of people didn't go from Atlantic City to Smithville at that time, and she knew I was an ambassador for her."

The commission launched its bicentennial project at a dinner program held, of course, at Quail Hill on April 12, 1973. As chair, Ethel introduced the featured speaker, noted New Jersey historian John Cunningham. By this time, additional members had joined the commission, including Lillian Levy, a member of the New Jersey State Council for the Arts, and Adrian Phillips, hotelier and local history advocate. Ethel was in her element.

Then, in an unprecedented action, the Atlantic County Board of Freeholders designated Fred and Ethel Noyes honorary Freeholders in July 1973. The unique proclamation was made in recognition of the Noyeses' "tremendous effort in promoting the historic, social, cultural and commercial advantages of Atlantic County."

Amid the public acclaim, activity of another sort was taking place. "Inns' Public Offering Successful" was the headline in the *Press of Atlantic City* on October 26, 1972. In fact, nothing could have been further from the truth. The story came out of Washington and stated, "The initial 80,000-share public offering of Historic Smithville Inns, Inc. was oversubscribed upon reaching the market Tuesday at $12 per share, according to Katz, Needleman and Co. Inc., a capital-based investment banking firm."

The stock offering was a last-ditch effort to stem a hemorrhaging cash flow. The banks no longer considered Smithville a good loan risk. "We couldn't get another loan," said Fiore. "We tried to raise half a million dollars, and the best we could do was $200,000. Her lines of credit were drying up."

Reviewing the Smithville, Inc. annual report dated March 25, 1973, accountant Joe Kaufmann elaborated, "Based upon cost, they only had $2,700,000 in buildings and land, but the debt was over $4 million. They were doing about $5 million of business most years and showing a bottom-line profit of $100,000, so they were working on 2 percent. That's a pretty tight margin. She should have been working on about 10 percent. Usually in this type of business, your salaries and wages will be around 25 percent, but it looks like they were at 34 percent.

"I guess one of the most interesting things to me," said Kaufmann, "was even though they did a great amount of business, they wound up making little or no profits, and their cash flows were very poor because she was continuously building. If she had cut the payroll, she probably would have been all right.

"On average, her accounts payable were two months behind. Some waited six months, and some were on a COD basis, I guess. I would say her accounts payable time was probably double what they should be in this business."

This situation was not a secret. Dick Butler remembered, "Jenkins was her plumber, Kiker was her roofer and Wagenheim sold her meat. She dealt locally—until they wouldn't deal with her anymore because she owed them too much money." Carl Fiore added, "The vendors had to get in line to get paid, and if you complained, you were fired. She would get someone new."

Ethel's brothers Ev and Hap Lingelbach knew of a restaurant in Florida that had raised money through a stock offering. For several years, they urged the Noyeses to take their business public. "Yes, it was the Kapok Tree, a restaurant in Florida where all this came about," said Kaufmann. "That was the model for them looking into this public offering with a firm in Washington, D.C. Based upon that, Ethel figured Smithville could go public."

Ethel resisted at first. But when she finally saw going public as a possible solution to a thorny debt problem, she pursued the project with a vengeance. According to the bartender Bo Burke, she pushed her employees to buy in. "Oh yeah, she was paranoid about that. She was trying to sell stock to the busboys. She would tell these people, 'You know, you should buy into the company.'"

The offering was filed with the Securities and Exchange Commission initially on July 21, 1972. It proposed 220,000 shares of common stock offered at $12 per share. The net proceeds were estimated at $2,200,000.

The prospectus clearly laid out the amazing growth that took place from 1952 to 1972 at Smithville. The land holdings grew from seven acres to over two thousand. The seating capacity for diners increased from forty-four in two small rooms to approximately two thousand in three "deluxe" restaurants, seven cocktail lounges and six bars. The company operated twenty-five individual gift and retail merchandise shops. On an additional area of approximately twenty-four acres, a Museum Village consisting of thirty restored Early American buildings was being constructed. There was a motel, the Jersey Traveler, and an airstrip. It was noted that the Department of Interior had designated Historic Smithville Inn as a historic site.

Although the *Press of Atlantic City* article proclaimed the offering a great success, the opposite was true. The sale of stock was no more successful than a finger in a leaking dike. According to Carl Fiore, "We filed this with the securities exchange and proposed offering 220,000 shares of common stock. Of course we never did achieve what we wanted out of that. I bought shares, a friend of mine bought shares; they were $12 a share. On the board we were allowed to buy in at $1 a share, but we couldn't sell it for two years, and by that time, well…"

Still Ethel couldn't stop. Camouflaged by frenetic activity, the reality of financial insolvency was unfolding. Many people knew pieces of the picture. There was a bounced paycheck here, an irate creditor there. But few grasped the total picture.

Betty Loveland at this time managed eight stores. In addition to the General Store, she was in charge of the cheese shop, the pewter shop, the gourmet shop, the barn, the tobacco shop, the candy store and the toy store.

Betty said, "We used to have meetings, the store managers. We each got a monthly report on how much we made. We had to pay our help, our heat, electricity and for our merchandise. The last report I got in 1971 on the General Store, we had cleared $65,000 for the year. Mr. Cherry gave us those reports; he was my boss then."

Then Mr. Cherry came and told Betty that Ethel wanted to see her order books. Betty's stores were low on inventory, so Betty grudgingly took over her books to Ethel's office. Betty had copies of the orders, and Irma Offner confirmed it. In fact, Ethel had the orders in her drawer. Ethel was deluding herself. She tried to blame Betty for not placing orders and keeping her stores stocked. In fact, it was Ethel herself who did not place the orders because she was so delinquent with the vendors that they would no longer fill them.

Betty had the same experience at trade shows. Ethel told Betty to purchase what she wanted, and then Ethel walked away. The vendor would say, "We'll take your order, but you won't get it until the last bill is paid."

At the same time debt was creeping higher at Smithville, the national outlook was changing from the optimism of the 1950s. By the early 1970s, the once-vigorous economy began to experience inflation.

The gas crisis was a shock to auto-dependent Americans, who now had to wait in long lines and pay high prices at the fuel pump. Road trips were curtailed and travel plans cancelled. Schools and offices shut down early to save energy, and factories cut production and laid off workers. No single factor did more to cause soaring inflation in the 1970s than the skyrocketing price of energy.

Historic Smithville Inns, Inc. was hit hard by inflation and the energy crisis. New Yorkers and Philadelphians who had driven to the famous restaurant for Sunday dinner now changed their plans and stayed closer to home. Gas prices were up, and the value of the dollar was down. Pride and enthusiasm for America and her history wavered.

Ethel was determined that Smithville appear in full operation even if there were few patrons to serve. Business was especially slow during the winter months when the volume was less than half the summertime.

Glenn Kennedy, maitre d' at the elegant and intimate Lantern Light Inn, remembered discussions with Ethel about the payroll. "Well, we had our off days. And then on snowy nights she brought people to work that should not have been brought to work. The payroll ticked on, and I kept trying to tell her, 'Mrs. Noyes, lay the people off in the winter, we are in the gas crisis, we are not going to get the business that you think we are going to get.' She thought people would come in anyway. You have to curb payroll. At one point, our payroll was $47,000 a week."

Keeping the restaurants operating at full tilt also meant paying utility bills, bankrolling the cleaning and maintenance staff and keeping the kitchen and storage areas stocked.

As business was declining, the competition was increasing. The biggest competitor for volume of business was Zaberer's Restaurant. Ed Zaberer, a restaurateur who had worked in Atlantic City hotels, built an eating establishment near the Atlantic City Racetrack on the Black Horse Pike, about a half-hour drive west of Atlantic City going toward Philadelphia. The enormous building was modeled on a European ski chalet. Zaberer's "zaberized" drinks and meals were also enormous, one and a half to two times as large as those served in other restaurants.

Bo Burke had firsthand knowledge. "I worked there for ten years prior to Smithville. It was a 'junky competitor' in the sense that Fred and Ethel were very elegant in what they did. This guy Zaberer put out wonderful food, but he had kind of a circus atmosphere, cheap, you know. Zaberer's might do three thousand to four thousand meals everyday, with 135 waitresses, which was quite a volume of business. Smithville had the same number of waitstaff, but fewer customers per wait team. Everything was low-keyed as opposed to the rapidity at Zaberer's. But when the china and glass show came to Atlantic City, they had all their parties at Smithville because of the elegance."

Glenn Kennedy remembered Ethel's increasing obsession with Zaberer's Restaurant. "She was very jealous of Zaberer's, very jealous. She and I had more run-ins about that. She would say to me, 'Glenn, go out to Zaberer's and count the cars in the parking lot.' I would say, 'Mrs. Noyes, what are you trying to prove? They probably told all the employees to park out there.'"

The competition caused the Noyeses to make some changes in their business operations, and not for the better. Many people thought the mass-produced meals churned out of the Quail Hill commissary did not compare in quality with the dinners previously cooked at Smithville Inn and personally inspected and often tasted by Ethel herself.

Even the gourmet Lantern Light Inn changed. When Glenn Kennedy started working there in 1965, it became a prosperous successful 'tuxedo-type' restaurant. "We had white glove service and seated people up to eleven o'clock at night. We were cooking at the table, preparing Caesar salad, steak Diane, steak tartar, crepe Suzette, the works. The wine had proper time to breathe. Everything was just as the customer wanted it. Even though the check was larger, the turnover was quite slow. Ethel said you have to get more volume of business. So, she took our menu away and made it the same as the Inn. We lost a lot of customers then. They started going to Seaview, places where they could get that type of food and service."

There were other signs of cracks in the façade. Sometimes payroll checks were not covered. Bo Burke said, "We as employees would be saying in the winter, when is it going to get busy? We workers would hear trickles of financial strain from her people. 'Oh, she's really complaining about money now.' A couple times a year, my paycheck would bounce. Then I would tell Ethel's brother-in-law, Bob Muller, and he was almost in tears. It was like a knife in his heart to hear that."

Chapter 12

AND THE BEAT GOES ON

Theft, a common problem in the restaurant business, was another leak in the cash flow. Rapid growth at Smithville made the situation even worse. As more employees were hired and operations became more complex, it became impossible for even the omnipotent Ethel to be everywhere all the time. She just didn't have enough family to go around. In the area of security, Ethel was assertive and precedent setting. This was due in part to her longtime relationship with local detective Al Black. Al's father, Richard, had been a "very dear friend of Mrs. Noyes when she worked on the ration board in Egg Harbor," said Al. Al joined his father, who had been chief of the Atlantic City Vice Squad before he retired, in the Black International Detective Agency in the 1950s.

Ethel probed Al about his detective agency because she was concerned about the safety and welfare of her customers as well as employee theft. Al recalled, "We had a timekeeper that punched the employees in and out of the doors. And we had guards so that if anyone came out with a bag, or came in with one, it was checked. We did stop a lot of employees; you see they all had to go out the one door.

"Mrs. Noyes was way ahead of her time," Al said. "She wanted people to know that if they parked their cars and walked around that they could feel safe. We had patrols on the grounds to make sure that people could walk around and not be terrorized or vandalized. She believed that prevention was worth it.

"If I had an idea or she did, we would work it out. She used to say, 'Let me tell you, things are going to get worse in this country, not better.'"

Al pioneered the use of men with dogs, walking the premises and in a patrol car, at Smithville. The detective agency had people pose as customers in the shops just to make sure no one was stealing.

Even Fred was convinced to change. He had an old Thunderbird, and he would take his night deposits down to the Absecon Bank. Al admonished, "There is a lot of money in there from all the shops, why don't you get an armored car service? Someday someone is going to get you at night." At first Fred resisted, but eventually, they employed a service.

Constant activity and planning new projects diverted attention from the debt at Smithville. Al Black remembered several ideas Ethel discussed with him. She wanted to buy and restore the Oyster Creek Inn. She also wanted to build a hotel across from the Inn, next to Quail Hill. The hotel would provide cash flow and keep the customers on the Smithville property overnight so they could spend more at the shops and restaurants. Another attraction on the drawing board aimed at a new market segment was a golf course. Like the Williamsburg and Old Sturbridge Village models, Ethel envisioned Smithville as a comprehensive tourist destination.

While Ethel kept track of her world through a dozen eyes in her head, Fred kept pace in his own way. He continued to paint and carve, occasionally carving a frame for one of his paintings. He painted in his office. And he painted on the screened porch of their home that overlooked a spacious lawn that stretched down to the Mill Pond, a stopping place for migrating Canada geese, ducks and swans.

A "Selected Group of Paintings" was presented at Quail Hill in May 1970. A program for the show noted, "Fred Noyes is a businessman and has only limited time to expend on his art. But he prizes every available moment to express things as he sees them through painting. His work is characterized by generous strokes of brilliant color and a depth of sensitivity and understanding of the gentle, serene side of nature."

Fred's art got more animated and more abstract as the years went by. His painting *Busy River* is the culmination of this vigorous style. He also did paisley-like abstracts, reminiscent of his father's textile work. These paintings are alive with rich color and the swirling motion of plants and flowers bending and weaving with animated grace. The work is one-dimensional but bursting with a variety of buds, stamens, pistils and cross sections of seed pods and flowers in full bloom. The eye is kept busy following the energy of the painting, as if it were a living, growing thing.

In December 1972, Fred had a one-man show at the Newman Contemporary Art Gallery in Philadelphia. Many friends and peers from South Jersey attended the artist's reception.

Fred's art provided him with a happy and healthy outlet and probably lowered his blood pressure. And he could not eat while his hands were busy with his paintbrushes.

All Ethel's activities involved high energy, tension and keeping up appearances. Although she seemed superhuman, she had her limits. Her desire to do everything and be in several places at the same time led to stress and fatigue. Sometimes Ethel had two or three meetings, and she asked Mae Carrow to stand in for her. If Mae said she didn't have a dress, Ethel said, "Well, that's ok, I'll bring one in and you can just baste a hem in." Mae commented, "She just couldn't spread herself any thinner."

Mae wasn't the only one to fill in for Ethel. "When she was sick and in the hospital in the late '60s or early '70s, her sister Lois used to stand at the podium and hardly anyone knew the difference. She wore her hair like Ethel, and she dressed like her, especially the shoes. I called them the Dr. Lock orthopedics, with the tie-ups," recalled Dick Butler. "Ethel was very thin. She was having some stomach problems when she was hospitalized." Dick believed Ethel had an eating problem because she ate such small portions.

Ethel went to great lengths to conceal her health problems. She used their Rittenhouse Square apartment and from there made discreet doctors visits. When she had to spend time in Philadelphia for health reasons, she would make frequent calls to her office and staff so they would think she wasn't any further away than home. She didn't want anyone to think they could slack off because she was more than a few steps away.

"Another thing about Mrs. Noyes that I don't know if anyone has told you," said Glenn Kennedy, "She never missed appearing to be at Smithville every day. Even if she flew to Chicago to a hotel show, she caught the nine o'clock plane in the morning, and she was back at Smithville that night. She wanted people to think she never left Smithville. Even when she was in the hospital in Philadelphia for five days, a station wagon came from Port Republic to pick up two meals every night to pretend that she was home. She sent two of her nurses over to Smithville for a complimentary dinner, and one of them said to the waitress, 'You better treat us good because we have your boss in the hospital.' That was the first anyone knew of it."

The main problem troubling Ethel and taking a toll on her health was the Old Village. It was the focal point of Ethel's vision, but it was all cash out and no cash in.

According to Mae Carrow, there was too little preplanning and marketing. "They didn't have customer one. You don't do it that way. When you first pick up the hammer, that is when you need to start gathering your busloads of people. She did that all the time, she would open something and fortunately, generally, it would take off. So we were doing fine, but then let's do fine and catch up on our bills. But no, we would do fine and when this was finished, we would immediately start something else. She meant well, that was just how Ethel worked. People would talk to me about it, and I would just have to say, 'I know, I know.'"

It was decided to charge admission and use the sale of the craftspeople's products to offset some of the financial burden of the Old Village. But these policies were inconsistent, remembered Niki Giberson. "I think what happened was that when the Old Village first opened, they charged five dollars per person to get in. But for a family of five in the '70s, twenty-five dollars was a big amount. The following year, they changed it so it was free. I think they were hoping that the craftspeople would make it work. We were being paid with products that we produced that would help pay our salaries. But the problem with that was we were being paid to talk and to answer questions. Not everyone has the ability to mass-produce something and to be an entertainer at the same time. It seems like nothing was ever applied for long enough time to see if it would work. They were so worried that it wouldn't work they would change it."

As Al Black and his crew tightened their operations, some of the cost-cutting initiatives had a negative effect on the staff. Bo Burke resented that he had to sign in a book when he wanted to pass in or out at work. Burke complained, "Signing the book gave them permission to check everything I carried. Then there was a certain shelf area outside the check-in point. On the shelves were bushel baskets with broken china in them, all dated and labeled: December 7, $82.27 broken. This way the employees could see how much their accidents were costing."

What the employees were seeing was that their boss was anxious about money. Bruce Burrows, manager at Quail Hill, elaborated. "I've seen Ethel go through garbage late at night. She would roll up her sleeves and look for unnecessary waste. Sometimes if a steak got a little overcooked for one order, the chef would just throw it away instead of putting it aside for the next well-done order. But they never did it twice. She wanted to make everything good in there. If the butcher was taking meat off the bone, and she found a bone with a lot of meat on it, he just wasn't doing his job right."

When Bo Burke's pay rate was downgraded, he left Smithville. He was the exception, however. The others worried, but they stayed on. They would ask questions about the future of Smithville at staff meetings, and Ethel would assure them everything was fine. According to Irene Hartman, Ethel said, "As long as you see my hair in good shape, everything is not lost." They still had their jobs and still got paid, usually on time. Wanting to believe Ethel, they thought things would work out.

Chapter 13

ABC Buyout

The End of a Dream

She always outspent what she had and that is what drove her. They almost went bankrupt.
—Clarence Hanselman

In 1973, Ethel Noyes was named one of the top ten female executives in New Jersey. Carl Fiore nominated her, and the honor was bestowed by Governor Cahill.

At the same time, American Broadcasting Company was looking for businesses to acquire. Prompted by Ethel's recognition, the ABC executives made a trip to meet her and look at Smithville. Carl Fiore remembered, "They came down and looked the place over. The chairman was impressed, and he asked his president what could be done with it. It was just an ordinary visit to see what she was doing, but they were very impressed and they wanted it. She was up to here with bills, so she decided maybe she would do it."

It was a stroke of good fortune that ABC came forward with an offer to buy Smithville. The place was over $3 million in debt and on the verge of bankruptcy. "Fred told me himself, they almost went down," said Clarence Hanselman. Ethel would have preferred to remain boss, but she was smart enough to know it was time to put a stop to the negative cash flow and recoup her losses. For ABC, it was an opportunity to invest dollars with negative amortization and offset capital gains elsewhere in the company. "ABC approved a $1 million loan to Historic Smithville Inns, Inc., in return for a one-year option to purchase the complex," reported the *Press of Atlantic City* on February 12, 1974. The five-year loan was to be used to accelerate the expansion of the facility, which was valued at $9 million. Fred Noyes, president of Historic Smithville Inns, Inc., made the announcement jointly with Leonard H. Goldenson, ABC board chairman, and Elton Rule, president. If ABC exercised its option to buy, Historic Smithville Inns, Inc. stockholders would receive $7 per share for their stock. (The Noyeses owned 80 percent of the stock.) Mr. and Mrs. Noyes would continue as chief operating officers. Mrs. Noyes said they expected to open the Old Village by June 15.

The very next day's paper reported that ABC planned to exercise its option to buy. If the agreement was completed, Smithville would pay nothing on the loan for the first year, then $100,000 a year at 6 percent interest for the next four years, followed by a lump sum payment at the end of five years. Smithville would be run by ABC's Scenic and Wildlife Attractions subsidiary that owned and operated two tourist attractions in Florida and a wildlife preserve in Maryland. ABC's publicity director for the leisure division, Charles Franke, stated that the Noyeses had certain goals and that ABC would pursue them with the Noyeses in the driver's seat. "The décor of Smithville, the whole tradition of it, will in no way be violated by ABC. If anything, we will dedicate ourselves to expanding and accelerating the original plans. The Noyeses will oversee this dream they've had over the years." Franke further stated neither ABC nor the Noyeses approached each other directly on the agreement. "Actually, a third party initiated it," he said. "ABC Scenic and Wildlife Attractions has always been open to suggestions. Someone in the area knew about Smithville, and John E. Campbell, president of that subsidiary, said he'd like to hear more about it."

Five months later, ABC announced it had agreed to purchase all the assets of Historic Smithville Inns for $7 million and assume $2 million in liabilities. Mrs. Noyes said she and her husband would continue as operators and ABC would continue the historic restoration of the Old Village, which would be complete in six to eight weeks. Plans for a hotel were indefinitely postponed.

There were varying opinions as to how the sale of Smithville affected the Noyeses, especially Ethel. Some thought she was devastated, others relieved.

Ostensibly, the opportunity was pure relief. Al Black, who was having dinner with the Noyeses the night they got the message the deal was complete, said Ethel was ecstatic. "As it happened, I went over there and said to Fred and Ethel, 'I would like to take you both out.' I took them to the Palm Court at Howard Johnson's (now Caesars Hotel and Casino) for dinner. It was just a coincidence; I mean there was nothing set. I was sitting there with Fred and Ethel and my ex-wife. All of a sudden, the maitre d', Mr. Angelini, came over and said, 'Mrs. Noyes, you have a phone call.' When she came back, she said 'Thank God. I just sold Smithville to ABC. Mr. Goldenson just called, and the place is sold. Let's have a bottle of champagne.'"

Al Black's remarks reflected the thoughts of most of the community. "I was happy too. I always felt a lot of loyalty to her as a lot of other people did. Because when she made it, we made it. And if she wasn't making it, we couldn't make it. If she had gone down, we would have gone down. Let me tell you, when Ethel Noyes sold Smithville that was an end of an era. Smithville was her baby, but she was spending money to restore it faster than she could make it. She had so much respect for her help and the area. She cared more about that than herself."

Historian John Cunningham extolled Ethel for the move. "There was at the time a very strong belief that Ethel was more than a match for ABC. I knew a man who worked in public relations at ABC and thought they were going down to deal with a country girl. That country girl was totally up to dealing with them, and the Noyeses got a good price. I think that is one of the things she was able to manipulate. The sale was a crowning achievement. She was not overwhelmed by the businessmen in their $1,000 suits, by that or anything else in life. She had great respect for people, but I don't think she stood in awe of anyone."

But there was another side of the story. Marge Conover, wife of Ethel's cousin Floyd, didn't believe it was so easy for Ethel to give up the reins at Smithville. "It was devastating when she sold Smithville. That was her baby, all the years and hours she put into it. The debt was her fault though, and at the end the gas shortage hurt her. After ABC took over, she couldn't do what she did before. Her oldest brother, Ev, wanted her to go public long before she did. Maybe then she wouldn't have gotten into that mess. She couldn't be told what to do. It's a shame what happened."

Antoinette Olivier Smith also saw Ethel suffer because of the sale. Antoinette, known as Toni, was hired as a hostess for $1.25 an hour, and when she left twenty-eight years later, she was earning $2.95. Toni said, "Ethel cried when she had to sell Smithville. It was like she was kicked out of her own house, what she had built up all those years. It was like she was God, and all of a sudden she was not. I know I saw her crying."

Smithville pianist Bill Hoch affirmed Ethel's grief. "When she sold Smithville to ABC, my wife and I went over there and she was crying. I said to her, 'What's wrong?' She said, 'Bill, it is all gone, all that I have worked for is gone.'"

Ethel's sister Bertha said Ethel was a Type A personality. Although she had achieved a lot at Smithville, she was not able to complete her vision. Smithville was sold by necessity, not by choice. She left with a sense of failure; the opportunity to create a legacy was lost. She needed to prove herself and to be a complete success in her own eyes. Her health continued to be affected by stress and possibly depression.

Ethel may have had mixed emotions, but selling Smithville caused Fred no pain. "It didn't bother me at all. I had a $3 million mortgage. I left that behind too."

Herbert Rothenberg handled the contractual agreement between the Noyeses and ABC. It appeared the terms were satisfactory to both parties. Joseph Kaufmann was involved in the negotiations and stated, "That was an honor point in my life."

Certainly it was honorable to pay off outstanding debts. Shareholders in Smithville Inns were paid. "She made sure people didn't lose money," said Carl Fiore. "They didn't make any, but when she sold out to ABC she paid people out, she felt an obligation. Eventually everybody got paid."

Not much changed at Smithville right away. Most employees stayed on, including restaurant manager Bruce Burrows. According to the contract, he recalled, Ethel was the president and Fred the vice-president. Ethel reported directly to the head of ABC. "She would be in complete charge, just the same, and everyone was fine about it. We were all thinking everything is great."

But everything wasn't great. Ethel wasn't used to being accountable to anyone, even the head of ABC. Its business philosophy was very different than her own. Ethel confided to Mae Carrow, "I don't think ABC has ever heard of George Washington." Carl Fiore put it succinctly when he said, "ABC looked at it as a money-making operation; for Ethel, it was her lifestyle."

Ownership may have changed at Smithville, but community recognition of the Noyeses never ceased. As the nation moved closer to the bicentennial celebration, Ethel's prominence increased. Governor Brendan T. Byrne appointed her as one New Jersey's delegates to the reconvening of the First Continental Congress in Philadelphia.

In November 1974, the Greater Mainland Chamber of Commerce honored the Noyeses for their efforts in preserving South Jersey's colonial heritage. The dinner, attended by more than three hundred distinguished members, was held at the Historic Towne of Smithville. Atlantic County solicitor Irving Lilienfeld was the toastmaster.

"I remember twenty-three years ago," said Lilienfeld, "this place was a broken-down building, no floor, no roof. Why, no respecting dog would even go and do his business there.

"I remember Fred Noyes before he became famous. The most exciting thing he did on a Saturday night was to go down to the gas station, which was in Wading River, and jump up and down on the hose to hear the bell ring.

"Well, needless to say, they've come a long, long way. The only thing I have to say is, God bless Fred and Ethel Noyes. It's a magnificent thing they've done.

"Don't forget, they employ some six hundred people at Smithville. A lot of them senior citizens and a lot of them young people too. But for Fred and Ethel Noyes, there would be a lot of unemployment in this county."

The featured dinner speaker was WPVI sports commentator Joe Pellegrino, an interesting choice considering ABC owned WPVI. It was Pellegrino's first visit to Smithville, and he found the extensive complex "breathtaking." He said the Noyeses were held in high esteem outside the area. "They are legendary figures any place on earth where people are concerned with their heritage. These two have preserved a lot of the past for generations ahead."

The Noyeses were given a standing ovation, a plaque and three "special gifts," a paint-by-the-numbers set for Fred, a coupon for one free cheese sirloiner at Gino's and a set of Lincoln Logs. "You know, it's really true about these logs," said Fred, lifting the tin of Lincoln Logs in his hand. "I remember Ethel and I were riding along one day, and we saw a chimney sitting in a field, and my wife stopped and said, 'That's got possibilities.'"

Opening ceremonies at the Old Village took place on May 3, 1975. Governor Brendan T. Byrne pulled up in a coach with a team of horses at the main entrance followed by the Absegami High School marching band playing "The Battle Hymn of the Republic." Byrne headed an entourage of local and state officials who paid tribute, read proclamations and presented flags and honorary degrees to Fred and Ethel. Seated on a portable stage in the chilly morning air, the Noyeses heard themselves proclaimed part of the state's history.

"It's a beautiful honor," said the willowy Mrs. Noyes in thanks for the honorary bachelor of arts degree conferred on her and her husband before a crowd of several hundred adults and children. Dr. Richard Bjork, president of Stockton State College, said of the Noyeses, "They aren't college educated. They are self-educated."

Following a luncheon, ABC's Scenic and Wildlife Attractions division president John E. Campbell addressed the group. He said the new thirty-eight-structure Old Village added another $1.5 million worth to the purchase ABC made the previous year. He estimated the furnishings inside the restored homes, schools and shops would double the value of the park. "Those antiques haven't been appraised in twenty years," Campbell said. "The corporation intends in our long-range plans to construct a $3 million lodge here with a nine-hole golf course, indoor and outdoor swimming pools, tennis courts and a tennis clinic."

Governor Byrne concluded, "Smithville's Old Village will help people remember and realize the great contribution of our state during the 1800s. Fred and Ethel Noyes have become part of that history."

The more ABC analyzed how to make Smithville and the Old Village profitable, the more it diverged from Ethel's original concept. With an eye to making money by making it easier for visitors to get from the Old Village to the restaurants and shops, management decided to build a bridge across Lake Meone. Ethel had butted heads with ABC before over various things, but this decision was the proverbial straw that broke the camel's back. Manager Bruce Burrows remembered the occasion well.

"I stayed there as general manager after the purchase, and they had put in this flashy young fellow. He was very brash. And the public relations people had eighteen-year-old girls running around in the little skirts for big ads in the paper. Then Ethel came in one day and said, 'What are they doing out back?' They were building a bridge across the lake. Well, she could not work for somebody like that. And neither could I. That time she just came right in and quit."

"They've ruined my village," Ethel told Gary Giberson. And that's when she left.

From that point on, things happened fast.

"Nobody could supervise Mrs. Noyes," Glenn Kennedy remembered. "Fred told me they gave her $100,000 severance pay and twenty-four hours to get out of the place. They were packing their personal items in the middle of the night and hoping to God that they did not forget anything. I witnessed that, I helped them. So I know it was done as a very unfavorable separation."

But the hastily drawn separation documents may have favored the Noyeses in the end, because some standard stipulations were apparently overlooked.

"Noyeses Announce Retirement from Smithville," was the public version of the ABC-Noyes separation reported in the *Press of Atlantic City* on August 28, 1975. Smithville public relations director Sidney Ascher handled the news release masterfully. "The parting was amicable," stated Ascher. "Mr. and Mrs. Noyes have been thinking about it for some months now. Discussion has been going for weeks and weeks, and they've always stalled off on the announcement. Now people are calling me and trying to think of diabolical reasons. There was no shuttle diplomacy."

ABC's John Campbell, president of the Scenic and Wildlife division, said a new general manager would be appointed in the near future. According to ABC, "Mr. and Mrs. Noyes said they plan to devote much of their time to the Mr. and Mrs. Fred Winslow Noyes Foundation, which, among other philanthropic activities, is involved in the planning of a museum to be located in Atlantic County. The museum will be to display art work and artifacts of historical significance to southern New Jersey, including Mr. Noyes' extensive decoy collection."

"They've worked hard all these years, never really taken a day off. They've earned their relaxation," said Ascher. "Knowing them," he added, "They won't relax, really."

Chapter 14

A MOST ELEGANT ENTERPRISE

THE RAM'S HEAD INN

Here at the Ram's Head Inn, Ethel was inspired by her girlhood visions of her Grandmother Priebs riding in a velvet lined coach on the way to the artist who would paint her portrait, later to hang in a museum in Dresden.

F red and Ethel could never be happy working for someone else. It was just one year from the time ABC bought Smithville to the time they announced their retirement. Those months gave Ethel time to redraw her dream and search out a business opportunity where she could again exercise her bountiful talents. And Fred was happy if Ethel was happy.

Ethel wanted to build again. Several properties were considered, but the one that seemed in the best location for the price was a family restaurant called the Dutch Barn on the White Horse Pike (Route 30) in Absecon, about nine miles from Smithville. The transaction was done through Ethel's youngest sister, Lois, and her husband, Bob Muller.

The separation contract with ABC stipulated the Noyeses couldn't go into business for one year. Lois recalled, "We were here on vacation from Venezuela. Bob and I bought the Dutch Barn property in our name because legally she could not do anything for a year. It was in our name, but of course, it was turned right back to Ethel and Fred when the time was up." An article in the *Press of Atlantic City* on January 7, 1976, stated, "Purchase of the Dutch Barn by the Noyeses had been alluded to in this column some three months ago, but its disclosure was premature at the time." This statement further muddles information about the sale. In any case, the Noyeses were ready to forge ahead. Or at least Ethel was, and Fred was along for the ride.

The property included the restaurant and four acres of land. The sale price was undisclosed. At the time of the purchase, the Dutch Barn was a three-hundred-seat family restaurant that served Pennsylvania Dutch cuisine. Previously it was the Black Steer and, prior to that, the Phillips Inn.

Dick Butler didn't like the Dutch Barn. "All the beauty was gone from what the inn had been originally. They had oilskin tablecloths, which smelled like wet diapers, and everything was served family style. They claim Ethel took home the separation papers from ABC to read and changed them. Originally it was that she was not allowed to open or run a restaurant within sixty miles, and supposedly she changed it by erasing the zero so it read six miles. The Dutch Barn was seven miles. So she got it, and a lot of the help went with her." According to Martin Wenig, comptroller at ABC, Ethel just bought where she did and no one objected. But there definitely was a noncompete clause in the separation contract with ABC.

The news article published the day after the settlement stated Mrs. Noyes was ebullient about the acquisition. "We enjoy being in business. We'll probably remain in business until we're ninety-nine. We are extremely pleased with the potential of the Dutch Barn. Certainly it is a smaller operation than our previous venture; however we have some very exciting plans. We will totally redo it. It will have a totally new and lovely look." The restaurant contained six individual dining rooms on the first floor and two small dining rooms on the second floor. The Noyeses did not plan to expand the restaurant but rather reduce the seating and have everything on the first floor. Asked if there were plans for the grounds, Mrs. Noyes smiled demurely and replied, "Yes, we are going to do something with them. We're going to do all we can to restore them to the way they were back when the Dutch Barn was Phillips Inn. The grounds were beautiful then. We hope to make the new restaurant a truly wonderful gathering place." The renovations would begin immediately. "We're using the same working team of contractors we've employed in all our past projects, with the exception of Roland Bonner of Pomona, who will serve as our new builder."

Roland Bonner was Ethel's second cousin. Ethel had confidence in him. Roland had worked full time with the head carpenter at Smithville, Bob Haviland, for two years. He then worked for other contractors, went into business for himself and finally worked out of the union in about 1975 because the economy was down.

One of the big union jobs was at the new Stockton State College dormitory in Pomona. Roland worked there with a union electrician and former high school classmate, Art Kurtz. Art and his wife, Sue, owned a corner lot in Port Republic two blocks from the Noyeses' home. After his union day job, Roland built the Kurtz house at night and on weekends. Ethel and Fred watched the house go up. They liked it so much that Ethel decided to get Roland to do some work for her and hired him to renovate an old barn at the Strickland farm on Old New York Road between Smithville and Port Republic.

Roland told her it was a piece of junk and to put a bulldozer to it. He said, "It was really in bad shape, half of it was rotted away. She spent a lot of money on it. I have no idea why she picked that barn, but I think she was going to let one of her nieces, Terri, live there. It had a stone foundation that was all falling down. It needed all new plates, siding, cedar shingles. I had to push the whole barn together. New beams, put the rafters back, rough sawn vertical siding. I hired one other guy. She spent $27,000 on that barn. It was almost winter when we finished, December of 1975. It was snowing. We were putting cedar shingles on in the snow, and I wanted to go skiing. That's when she told me she had a project for me if I wanted to do it." The Mullers had purchased the Dutch Barn, and the Noyeses were about to take possession.

Roland went to the Dutch Barn to look over the site with architect Rodney Williams's preliminary plans in hand. Rodney, his father and his brother were architects who had all worked with the Noyeses at Smithville over the years. Bonner gave Ethel an estimate for the project based on union workers at union wages, but it was vague because the plans were vague. Ethel was known to create as she went along. "We walked into one dining room one day, and she said, 'I want some beams in here.' Well, there was nothing on the plans, nothing. She said, 'I'm going to get Rodney over to draw a new set of plans.'"

"Noyes Restaurant Venture Being Treated 'Like Son'" was the headline in the *Press of Atlantic City* in September 1976. The reporter who visited the site said there was little trace of the Dutch Barn left, and the carpenters were midway through interior construction. The restaurant was slated to have 275 seats, fireplaces and skylights.

Speaking over the sound of hammering, Mrs. Noyes said, "We don't want to say too much now. We want it all to be a surprise. We want the customer to first find out what we are doing when he walks in here. A person can go out and hire a company to design a restaurant with a theme, but that's not what we wanted. We wanted to do it ourselves. It is like having a son."

The job was done in eight months. "Yeah, she was amazed," remembered Bonner. "She said she had never seen so much work done in eight months. She'd never seen men work as hard or do as much production as those union guys did. That was a good feeling."

The Noyeses needed a name for the restaurant. Ethel explained to a reporter for the *Asbury Park Press*, "We went over a long list of names for some time before we finally settled on Ram's Head Inn. It had a nice masculine sound. We didn't want a name that would give the impression this is a tearoom. Also, Fred was born under the sign of Aries, so it was appropriate."

Ethel worked nonstop to furnish the restaurant in a more elegant style than anything seen in the area. No expense was spared in choosing the finest Schumacher wallpaper and fabrics for window treatments and upholstery. Linens and china were top of the line. And interior painting was done and redone until the perfect shade was achieved by her patient cousin, Floyd Conover.

Cindy Mason-Purdie was working for the Atlantic County Cultural and Heritage Commission, and she remembered going to the new restaurant to get Ethel's signature on some paperwork for the commission. "She could really sit down and laugh at herself. That was something that helped her through things. I remember her telling me that it was hot during the summer. And it would be cooler if you didn't wear underwear. And that she was trying that, but it was not working."

Fred was always at the job site. He had his own office on the second floor (of the old inn) where he did his painting. At the time, he was doing abstracts in acrylics. Cindy remembered Fred as being like one of the smiling fish he painted. Fred never took himself that seriously, but he was serious about his art. He also worked on his decoy collection during the renovation of the inn, recalled Niki Giberson. "Every day he would bring a white canvas bag with about six decoys in it. He would sit there with a card table while they were building all around him. He would polish his decoys, and he would wax them, right there."

Bruce Burrows worked closely with Ethel while the Ram's Head was under construction. Bruce couldn't function after Ethel left Smithville. "I couldn't work, and ABC let me go about three weeks later. I called Ethel, and she said, 'Why don't you come down and we'll work out a schedule. I'll call ABC and make sure everything is alright.'

"Ethel tore that whole place apart," Burrows said. "She asked me to come to Philadelphia. 'How is six o'clock tomorrow morning? We'll have lunch up there and spend the day.' She worked through the contractor's department at John Wanamaker's. My job was to take a yellow pad and record whatever she looked at and liked. Pretty much she'd make up her mind by the next morning. She loved every moment of that, buying new furniture, setting the rooms up. We worked seven days a week. She went to New York City quite a few times for the linen, the china, the silver, the light fixtures, tables, chairs, everything. She did a beautiful, beautiful job. It was entirely different, it was magnificent; it was in the Federal period instead. It was not the same in any way as Smithville, and she loved it. She worked harder than ever."

The Noyeses purchased land adjacent to the Dutch Barn in 1976 and 1977 with the assistance of real estate agent Helene Walls. Helene had known the Noyeses since 1959 through her mother, Carolyn Walls, who was the organist in the Great Bay Room at Smithville for seventeen years.

From the point of view of a real estate agent, Helene thought Fred and Ethel were a good team. "They would see everything together. Fred was a good trader. He had survival instincts he learned from nature when he lived in the Pine Barrens." Helene remembered wryly one time they were walking along, and there was a snake on the ground. Fred said, "He moves pretty well for not having any legs."

Helene observed, "Ethel took her sweet old time renovating the Ram's Head." The result was elegant. Only one section of the original building dating back to the 1920s was retained. Four fireplaces were added. There were three dining rooms, a taproom, a parlor, a large foyer, a small banquet room and a gallery. Up several steps from the entrance foyer, the Gallery gave guests a taste of art before their gourmet dining experience. The room was designed to display the work of regional and other artists. A skylight ran the length of the ceiling, which had a bank of spotlights to properly light the paintings. More natural light came through large windows that lined one side of the room and overlooked the garden. Dinner guests were encouraged to linger in the Gallery, enjoy a cocktail and piano music and perhaps purchase a painting hanging on the wall.

Each room had a theme. One dining room had an Oriental look, picking up its orange and brown motif from a large painting of a Thai princess. A small garden dining room was decorated in shades of green, yellow and white and featured hanging plants and white bamboo furniture. The taproom, called the Study, had a masculine atmosphere complete with bookshelves, a spacious fireplace, black wrought iron and abundant dark wood. At the end of the U-shaped bar was a large nude painting selected by Fred.

The opening of the Ram's Head Inn was as quiet and purposeful as Ethel's speaking voice. Interested friends, associates and former employees had been stopping by for months to check out the progress. "People that followed her knew," said Bruce Burrows. "We turned on the lights one night in November, and we were open. She wanted no publicity, nothing, nothing, nothing." There was never a formal "opening" of the Ram's Head Inn. Its business simply evolved. Hence the contract with ABC was not broken.

A number of employees were summoned to work at the new establishment. But as usual, family was the mainstay. Bertha and Lois and Bob Muller's daughters, Chris and Terri, were brought on board. The Noyeses especially valued Chris Muller's talent. Mae Carrow said, "Chris Muller was a dead ringer for Ethel Noyes, and she was just as sharp. She was an inspirational person to be around."

Ethel knew exactly who she wanted and how to use their talents. John Cherry had been manager of the shops at Smithville. "He was very dynamic, just bounding with energy," recalled Bruce Burrows. Ethel told Burrows, "Get John Cherry." Burrows asked why, because there were no shops at the Ram's Head Inn. There was a little shop in the coatroom during the summer when people did not need to check their coats. But it was small, and Bertha took care of that. When Burrows called, Cherry said, "Just tell me what to do, and I'll do the best I can." He was put in the storeroom as manager of inventory and purchasing. John knew merchandising, and Ethel knew how to keep her valued employees.

Others couldn't wait to be called. Earl Robinson, trusted and talented chef, left about the same time as Burrows. There was no kitchen at Ram's Head yet, so he went to the new casino, Resorts International. Nor was there a Historic Village at the Ram's Head Inn. So Gary Giberson went to Wheaton Village, a recreated turn-of-the-twentieth-century glass manufacturing community in Millville, New Jersey. Without even putting in an application, he was hired as a wood carver on the basis of his reputation.

Mae Carrow was another employee Ethel wanted back. Mae said, "We were supposed to have lunch one day. She was very busy over there with the Ram's Head Inn. They were to the point that in a few days they would be open. She said, 'Mae, I am just so busy, let's just have lunch here.' So the chef was setting up the kitchen, and he prepared us a delicious lunch. People would come in, and Ethel would say, 'You know, we're not technically open, but we have some extra food. If you want to have what we are having, you are perfectly welcome to stay.' More cars came, and we had so many people stopping that we never had open house. Money was just walking through the door. This was in November. People started asking for gift certificates for Christmas. We hadn't really made up our minds about gift certificates yet, how we wanted it, because we still hadn't opened! So when they wanted gift certificates, I sat down at the typewriter and made gift certificates. We sold so many, we had people waiting."

Mae was again working in the area of public relations doing promotions and press releases. "I was setting up in the kitchen at Ram's Head for pictures for a magazine. We had to be beautiful. We had to put the hose back, and put the dirty kettles on the dish table, all this stuff. Then, oh my gosh, there was a fight. One of the cooks and one of the waiters got into words, and the words got heated. And you don't tell Fred, because Fred only puts more fuel on the fire. He doesn't know how to cool down a situation. I stood outside the kitchen door, and Ethel walked right into the midst of it and she said, 'You know I have no choice but to let you go. One of you has to go, and I can't lose that cook.' This was an older man she was telling this to. So the older man immediately left the job. The cook spoke up. He went to see Ethel Noyes, and he said, 'I'm sorry for what has happened. Don't fire that man, it will never happen again.' So, he was back by that evening serving dinner."

Steve Calvi also came over to the Ram's Head Inn as a waiter. He admired Ethel's poise under pressure. "Once a man came up to the podium and told Mrs. Noyes that he was a personal friend of 'Mr. and Mrs. Noles,' not Noyes, but Noles, and he wanted to be seated immediately. Ethel did not react at all. She said quietly, 'I'm sorry, sir, but I have my orders and I'm going to have to just put you on the list.' It was hysterical."

A few months after the Ram's Head Inn opened, however, ABC got an injunction for the Noyeses to cease and desist hiring ABC employees from Smithville. Burrows said, "Then we had to start looking for servers. Anybody who was working at the Inn we could not hire."

A year after the Ram's Head Inn started welcoming dinner guests, the inn was named one of the ten "New Good Neighbors" for 1977 by the *New Jersey Business Magazine*. The other businesses cited for the awards were large corporations that employed thousands, such as Prudential Insurance Company. In comparison, the Ram's Head Inn was a moderate-sized restaurant, and its nomination to the select ten by the Southern New Jersey Development Council was impressive. Ethel was serving on the board of the development council at the time.

"When is a restaurant not just a restaurant? When it's a creation of Fred and Ethel Noyes," began the article in *New Jersey Business Magazine* in December 1977. The Ram's Head Inn was chosen as an economic good neighbor because it employed 165 people from the area and paid over $18,000 in salaries weekly and another $19,000 to purchase food and beverages locally. It did an impressive amount of business with area contractors, such as landscapers, musicians, cleaners, security personnel and building equipment specialists.

Fred and Ethel were looking for a bookkeeper, and they turned to Carl Fiore for help. Carl hired a bookkeeper from Washington, D.C. who came with the highest recommendations. Her name was Eleanor Miller. With the advantage of hindsight, Carl said, "I personally called and talked to the person who employed Eleanor in Washington. I suspect now the reason he gave me such a great recommendation was to get rid of her."

Bertha Lingelbach remembered Eleanor Miller well. "I don't know when exactly she got hired, not when they first opened. She was a bleached blonde, and I don't like to talk about people, but she was, well, the opposite of Ethel. She would be loud. And, oh, her voice, you could hear it all over, and she talked like Fred. Rough. She was big, not real trim. She did everything, and she could do everything. She tried to run things other than her job. She said she was in construction before she came here."

Eleanor and Fred hit it off immediately. He played into her hand like a puppy takes to a game of fetch. Eleanor's gusty attention to Fred was obvious to everyone. But Ethel, preoccupied with running the inn and numerous community commitments, ignored Eleanor, just as she had ignored the overwhelming debt at Smithville.

"Eleanor was very exciting to Fred," recalled Niki Giberson. "She was feisty. She was everything that Ethel wasn't. She had a mouth on her. She gambled. She reminded me of a female W.C. Fields. She loved to cook."

All the offices were upstairs in the Ram's Head Inn. Not long after Eleanor became ensconced as bookkeeper, however, Ethel moved her office downstairs. She didn't welcome interference or advice from an overbearing bookkeeper. And she had to get away from the loud and constant banter between Fred and Eleanor.

But Ethel could not get away from the fact that Fred was enchanted with Eleanor. It seems odd that Ethel would give way to a woman she found uncouth and who was striking up an uncomfortably close relationship with her husband. She wanted Fred to be happy, but this time she gave too much. Fred's flirtations were usually harmless, but Fiore said, "He was really crazy about this one."

Ethel finally couldn't take the relationship between Fred and Eleanor anymore. Fred was "too involved" and openly attentive to Eleanor. There was only room for one strong woman in Fred's life. Ethel went to Carl Fiore and told him, "Eleanor is too cozy with Fred. I'm going to have to fire that girl, Carl. And since you hired her, you are going to have to fire her."

Chapter 15

THE IRONIC START
OF A LEGACY

THE NOYES MUSEUM

Irony: Incongruity between what might be expected and what actually occurs.

E thel constantly badgered Fred about his health, especially his eating habits, but ironically, it was she who had the more serious health problems. Heart disease was in her family. Caroline Lingelbach, Ethel's mother, was sixty-seven when she died of a heart attack. Her younger brother Hap also died of a heart attack.

Ethel had been symptomatic for years. She always carried nitroglycerine, and once in a while she would pop a nitro, recalled her sister Lois.

Ethel may also have suffered from low vital capacity, the relationship between lung capacity and the amount of air that can be expelled, a condition that affects the heart. Gary Giberson said, "She had a lung ailment that made it so she could not sleep in bed. She had a high-back wing chair that had a corner. She would use a little pillow, and she slept like that in the Green Room. This is later in life. She could not lay down horizontally."

Others were aware of Ethel's increasing health problems. Cindy Mason-Purdie was with Ethel on numerous occasions during the early days at the Ram's Head Inn. "I remember her telling me that she was suffering from bad indigestion. It was her heart. It was a symptom that could be angina. One time she got very upset at an Atlantic County Cultural and Heritage Advisory Board meeting. That was unheard of. We talked about it at the next meeting. We did think that maybe she was not feeling well. It was out of character."

Ethel's stress came from many quarters, public and personal. She drove herself as a businesswoman to the point of exhaustion. Her perfectionism would strain the strongest constitution.

On the personal front, Ethel was faced with ever-increasing worries. Never before had she feared Fred's involvement with another woman. Eleanor Miller, however, was seriously working her way into Fred's affections. It was hard to understand why Ethel endured the situation as long as she did.

Ethel distracted herself from her health and personal problems by focusing on her work. Now that the Ram's Head Inn renovation was complete, she was ready for a new project. It was her dream to make a permanent contribution to the preservation of the South Jersey's cultural history.

One place she accomplished this was with the Atlantic County Cultural and Heritage Advisory Board. In the late 1970s, the board, along with the Atlantic County Office of Cultural Affairs, published *The Atlantic County Cookbook*, a project near and dear to Ethel's heart. Cooking had been important to her ever since she was a little girl and watched her grandmother make sausage from an old German recipe. Cooking and recipes carried history with them. Ethel researched early American recipes for Smithville where chicken pot "pye" was featured on the menu. A loaf of homemade bread and a relish tray of apple butter, cottage cheese and cold corn relish were standard fare. Ethel surprised visitors to their Port Republic home when she put on an apron and headed to the kitchen.

"She loved to cook. She had a collection of over 250 cookbooks," said Gary Giberson. "I would go there in the morning, and she would be with her hair up and in her robe. She said go up and have breakfast with Fred, who would be sitting in his underwear on her bed. And she would cook us eggs. She knew how I liked my eggs, and I don't know how she did it, but she didn't use a form or anything. When she fried an egg it was just like this [demonstrates with hands], perfect. And the potatoes were all diced exactly right, with a little sprig of parsley. It was like going to a country inn or something."

Another place Ethel, together with Fred, pursued cultural preservation was in their hometown of Port Republic. A number of Port Republic residents, both old-timers and newcomers, were eager to preserve the local history, and the Noyeses were excited to help. They purchased the "Old Parsonage" on Main Street and loaned it to the newly formed Port Republic Historical Society. In return, the members spent time and sweat equity to help restore the building. They collected photographs and items of historic interest to put on display, and the Noyeses donated furniture and artifacts that had been stored in another historic house, the nearby Bowen property. On the day of the Old Parsonage Open House, some townspeople dressed in revolutionary period costume and gave tours. Baked goods, jams and jellies were made according to old-time recipes and sold to raise money for the society. This was in September 1978, and Cindy Mason-Purdie remembered, "Ethel planned to make beach plum jelly. It piqued my interest in South Jersey history when Ethel commented on the things she would make. We never got to do it. To this day, I still think of Ethel and beach plums."

Fred and Ethel also owned the Amanda Blake Store next door to the Old Parsonage on Main Street. Fred wanted to open the store as a decoy museum and have an annual art exhibit there. In the back was a big kitchen that Ethel started to refurbish with new ranges because she wanted to go there to cook and try out recipes.

It was the desire to build their own museum, however, that became Fred and Ethel's passion. To that end, the Mr. and Mrs. Fred Winslow Noyes Foundation was established on June 8, 1973. According to a history of the foundation, its mission was to form a broad-based museum that would reflect the specific interests of its benefactors. Ethel's interests were "primarily civic, historic and cultural," and Fred's "centered on his personal training as an artist and his interest in duck decoys." John Cunningham commented, "They had no children. I think the foundation became their children. I think she and Fred were very aware that they had to establish a future for themselves, a place of remembrance."

Lois Muller said, "You know, it wasn't Fred's idea to start a museum. Ethel was the one. It was her plan to preserve Fred's paintings and decoys and the history of the area. Her idea was a historic museum that keeps the younger generation in touch with the past. For example, 90 percent of people don't know what a cranberry scoop is; things like that, some of the things that are gone, they are no more."

The vision for the museum was threefold. First and foremost, the museum was to preserve the history of South Jersey by the display of artifacts, such as farming tools, photographs and documents.

Second, the museum would showcase local artists. Fred's prolific paintings would be on rotating display. Other artists, such as painter Tony Rudisill and glass paperweight maker Paul Stankard, as well as undiscovered artists, would be exhibited and promoted.

Third, the museum would house Fred's extensive decoy collection, one of the largest on the East Coast, numbering over 2,500 decoys made over a period of several hundred years. The collection was a tribute to the art and history of decoy carving. It included early working decoys that demonstrated simple lines and no frills but effectively attracted the hunted bird as well as contemporary display decoys that boasted exquisite feather carving and painting that looked soft enough to touch.

As the Noyeses continued to acquire parcels of land adjacent to the Ram's Head Inn, one option was to build a museum there. Typically, as she tossed around new ideas and plans, Ethel wanted someone to share the process. Gary Giberson remembered, "Ethel was getting ready. The inn had just opened, and she says, 'Okay, I got my Ram's Head Inn built now. Gary, we're going to start Fred's decoy museum. I want you and your wife to be part of this.'"

Another idea was for the Gibersons to live upstairs in the Amanda Blake Store while the museum would be downstairs. Gary would be the resident carver. "She wanted Niki and I to move upstairs to be caretakers. But Niki and I had a beautiful home. We had sheep that we were raising for the wool for Niki's spinning. We didn't want to live in the middle of town. But I said we could work something out. So she said, 'I'm going to have a meeting. I want to meet with you and Niki at the Ram's Head on Wednesday. And this was Saturday. So I said to Niki, 'My suit is awful. I'm going to buy a new suit.' So I went and bought a new three-piece suit and a shirt and a tie to match, the whole thing, the shoes. I bought everything for this meeting with Ethel."

On Tuesday, Ethel suffered severe back pains and lost consciousness. "Well," said Bert, "One night Fred called me. She had passed out at the house, and Fred couldn't find the phone number for the doctor. When she came to, she told him to call Bert. I called the doctor before I even left my house. It was a doctor in Absecon she used to go to every once in awhile. He came up for the first time to Port Republic. I went home after he came. I found out later that when he got there her pressure was way down. He should have put her in the hospital right then and there."

Gary continued, "So Wednesday come along, and she called me in the morning and she said, 'Gary, I'm not feeling too good. I'm going home. Fred's going to take me home, but I want you to come down and have dinner because it's all set up.' I said, 'No, no, Mrs. Noyes, I'll wait till you feel better.'

"The last time I saw Ethel Noyes alive she was coming home from the Ram's Head to go to the hospital the next day for tests. I never seen Ethel and Fred get romantic, and Fred was driving, and I came up Pitney Road and I followed them, I didn't want to pass them. Fred was driving about forty-five miles per hour, which is very slow for Pitney Road, I mean that is a sixty- to seventy-mile-per-hour jaunt through the woods. Ethel was sitting close to him, and then he put his arm around her and then she put her head on his shoulder. I just thought, wow, I had never seen them hug or embrace. It was romantic to me, and I remember getting a little wet-eyed.

"I said to myself, I've got to get a card for Ethel. I went down to the mall and started going through all the cards. I thought, it really has to say something, because when Ethel sent a card it was perfect. So, I find this perfect card for her, and I sign it Gary and Niki and I mail it."

Why didn't Ethel go to Philadelphia at this point? Why didn't she go when she first started having serious problems with pain and loss of consciousness on Tuesday? Philadelphia was just an hour car ride away, and her physician, Dr. Ginsberg at Temple, was there.

Glenn Kennedy reflected, "Mrs. Noyes did some things that were not in line with her stature. I mean, why did she have her heart surgery here? It shouldn't have been here. She went to Philadelphia to have her hair done every Thursday. In my opinion, the operation should have been up in Philadelphia."

Ethel went to the hospital, the Mainland Division of the Atlantic City Medical Center, on Friday and was admitted for testing. She was advised to have a pacemaker operation on Saturday, and she could be back at the inn the following week. Ethel agreed, and a temporary pacemaker was implanted on Saturday. In shock and completely unable to deal with the situation, Fred was also hospitalized.

The next day was Sunday, January 21, 1979. Gary Giberson remembered, "It was Super Bowl Sunday. So I'm listening to the radio, and it comes on the radio, 'Ethel Noyes dies of a massive coronary heart attack.' I turned the radio off, and I went out in the kitchen and Niki was standing there. I was crying. Niki said, 'What is the matter?' I said, 'Mrs. Noyes is gone. She died, Niki.' Niki said, 'Oh no, what happened?' She gave me a big hug. I told her it was a massive coronary. I went outside and walked around and looked at the pine trees, and I thought, oh my God."

Gary Giberson was among many who were shocked by Ethel's sudden death at 4:10 that Sunday afternoon. Constantly in motion and oriented to the future, she had created the impression of eternal strength. It seemed Ethel's energy and ideas would never end. Glenn Kennedy voiced a common thought when he said, "I think she died prematurely. I pictured her running things until she was ninety-two."

Bertha was the only immediate family member in the area when Ethel died. She remembered, "That night I had to call my brothers and sister—all in Florida. I was all alone that night."

The Noyeses' good friends Jack and Virginia Lamping went to the home in Port Republic about 7:00 p.m. on Monday. At that time, they learned from a neighbor, Mrs. Larry Smith, that Fred was still in the hospital. The family made the arrangements for a viewing at 10:00 a.m. on Wednesday, January 24, at the Jeffries and Keates Funeral Home in Northfield. Services, conducted by the Reverend Milton Collins of Port Republic, were to follow at 11:00 a.m.

Ethel would never tell her age. In keeping with this preference, obituaries and articles written at the time of her death did not refer to her age or birth date.

"Ethel Noyes, founder of Smithville Inn," was the bold-print headline of the feature obituary in the *Trenton Times* on January 22, 1979. Reporter Lee Pasternack noted Ethel Noyes died Sunday while negotiations were underway for the second sale of the historic Smithville site for a reported $20 million. The obituary erroneously reported that she was in her seventies. Ethel was sixty-seven years old when she died.

"Ethel Noyes Dead," headlined an extensive article in the *Press of Atlantic City.* "She was a woman with great vision," said Sidney Ascher. "She was able to look at a piece of vacant land and envision just what it would be like when it was completely developed. Ethel Noyes loved South Jersey and never wanted to leave. A woman with her wealth could travel around the world, but this was the place she loved. This is a terrific loss to the entire area."

The following day, many more came forward to praise Ethel. Governor Byrne said, "With her historical expertise, she left a mark on the future by preserving the past."

Galloway Township manager Joseph Picardi added, "She left an indelible imprint on a lot of people and on the area that can be seen. The area will always be a better place because she was here. I lost a personal friend, and the area lost a great person in Ethel Noyes." Ethel's numerous contributions and affiliations were listed again and again, filling columns of newspaper space.

"Even the skies opened up to weep for Ethel," said a visibly shaken Sidney Ascher at the funeral. "People have flown in from all over the country. She was a grand lady. There will never be another Ethel Noyes." More than five hundred people braved a stinging, wind-driven sleet to attend the viewing and funeral services. For more than an hour prior to the service, umbrella-toting mourners waited patiently outside the funeral home before slowly filing past the open casket, surrounded by dozens of ornate floral arrangements. After extending condolences to the family, they slowly approached the coffin, some weeping openly, others sobbing silently as they said goodbye with their prayers.

Glenn Kennedy recalled later, "Yeah, I really missed her, she was a leading lady. I felt very bad at the funeral, especially when they shut the door on those hundred people that couldn't get in. It was a snowy, blustery, icy day, and Fred had been in the hospital. I think they just brought him out for the service. There were so many people lined up, but Bob Muller and Lois had a time that the funeral was to be and they just shut the door. They turned away all those people, and some were probably coming from Trenton and didn't even get to pay last respects. I would have extended it. Such a premature death you know. She built such a beautiful town and then turned around and built a beautiful restaurant, and they are still here."

As it was, mourners filled every seat and spilled into the aisles of the chapel at the Jeffries and Keates Funeral Home.

The *Press of Atlantic City* reported, "'She knew every stick and every grain of sand in the area,' said the Reverend Milton Collins of the Port Republic Methodist Church. 'She created an institution that's become a blessing to many folks.'

"Toward the end of the twenty-minute service, a dry-eyed Mr. Noyes opened his eyes and stared straight ahead, his gaze fixed intently on his wife."

The day was a vivid memory for Gary Giberson. "I ended up wearing my new three-piece suit to her funeral. Mr. Noyes was so drugged up; he was just like zombified. It was the biggest funeral I ever attended in my life. They asked me to be pallbearer. It was unbelievable. I thought, that's it, they will never build Fred's decoy museum."

Following the services, a lengthy funeral procession, including dignitaries, politicians, business associates, employees and friends, made its way from Northfield to the Absecon Presbyterian Church. The family stood close during a brief graveside service and burial.

Eulogies for Ethel continued well after the funeral. "Ethel Noyes, Inspiration to Many" was an article by the *Press of Atlantic City* writer Ed Hitzel. "She was among those who, for whatever reasons, know what they want and then make seemingly magical moves to get what they want. In reality, there is no magic involved, and there certainly is a lot of hard work mixed with intangibles like love and luck. Smithville was proof that any goal—whatever the scope—can be realized if a person wants it enough. Smithville was an inspiration to the watchers of the progress of the American dream. I first heard from Ethel Noyes several years ago when I was a teenager and won a Christmas lighting contest. She sent me a letter, congratulating me, as she no doubt did other winners. She didn't have to send the letter; no other business people did, and I never forgot it. I didn't know Ethel Noyes well. I didn't know what she was like at home or what she was like to work for. But I know her energy inspired me. And I know I'm not alone. And I know many people besides myself will miss that inspiration."

"Ethel Noyes, her legacy lives" was the caption on a photograph of Ethel published five days after she died. The *Press of Atlantic City* reporter Sonny Schwartz wrote that Ethel and Fred Noyes, although childless, had a fervent desire to help young people. "Fourteen years ago this desire was transformed into a fulfilled dream when they gave birth to the Noyes Foundation. More than $60,000 in scholarships was awarded to qualified students throughout state."

Ethel's living legacy was to be more than scholarships. She died unexpectedly on the eve of the start of a museum. Although Gary Giberson feared that her untimely death meant the end of the museum, he was mistaken.

"So about a week after the funeral, Niki and I were wondering what are we going to do, because I had already spoken to the Wheatons about leaving them. Mr. Wheaton was giving me a couple months leave of absence. I knew I wouldn't be back to him, but I was glad I didn't say anything.

"Fred calls us on the phone and says, 'I'm going to build more than a decoy museum. I'm going to build a big, beautiful museum as a tribute to Ethel.'"

Left to right: Fred, Ethel, Jack Lamping and Virginia Lamping at Fritz's one-man show at the Newman Contemporary Art Gallery, 1625 Walnut Street, Philadelphia, on December 6, 1972. *Courtesy of Jack Lamping.*

Left: Ethel at the Newman Gallery reception for Fred's one-man show on December 6, 1972. *Courtesy of Tony and Fran Coppola.*

Below: Ethel and Fred at the Mainlander of the Year dinner at Quail Hill on November 17, 1974. *Courtesy of Gary and Niki Giberson.*

Top: The Dutch Barn, the restaurant Ethel and Fred bought and converted to the Ram's Head Inn. *Courtesy of Roland Bonner.*

Bottom: Fred at the construction site of the Ram's Head Inn in 1976. *Courtesy of Roland Bonner.*

Above: Ram's Head
Inn today, owned and
operated by the Knowles
family. *Photo by Joe Courter.*

Left: Herbert Rothenberg,
Esq., 1973. *Courtesy of the
Noyes Museum of Art.*

Right: Carl R. Fiore, 1973. *Courtesy of the Noyes Museum of Art.*

Below: Stained-glass art behind the altar designed by Fred Noyes in the chapel dedicated in memory of Ethel Noyes at the Atlantic City Medical Center, Mainland Division, Jim Leeds Road, Galloway Township. *Photo by Joe Courter.*

Above: Niki Giberson and Fred cataloguing decoys at the Noyes home in Port Republic. There were several thousand decoys and early American artifacts, so this project took many long days, circa 1980. *Courtesy of Gary and Niki Giberson.*

Left: Fred and decoys outdoors at home in Port Republic. *Courtesy of Gary and Niki Giberson.*

Bertha Lingelbach at Fred's birthday party in April 1981. *Courtesy of Gary and Niki Giberson.*

Eleanor Miller behind Fred at his infamous seventy-sixth birthday party on April 22, 1981. *Courtesy of Gary and Niki Giberson.*

Above: Helene
Walls with Fred at
his seventy-sixth
birthday party, April
22, 1981. *Courtesy of
Gary and Niki Giberson.*

Left: Anne Fabbri,
founding director of
the Noyes Museum
of Art, 1982–91.
*Courtesy of the Noyes
Museum of Art.*

Top: The Noyes Museum of Art of Stockton College, 2013. *Photo by Joe Courter.*

Bottom: The Noyes Museum of Art, looking down the central gallery to Lily Lake when first opened in June 1983. *Courtesy of Paul Cope.*

Gary Giberson demonstrating decoy carving at the Noyes Museum, gallery 2, 1983. *Courtesy of Gary and Niki Giberson.*

Opposite, top: Fred painting on the porch at home (the Franklin Inn) in Port Republic. *Courtesy of Jack Lamping.*

Opposite, bottom: Fred's painting *Busy River*, from the collection of Gary and Niki Giberson. *Photo by Joe Courter.*

Top: Fred, fishing and satisfied. *Courtesy of Gary and Niki Giberson.*

Bottom: Fred with his dog Lee Mackey. *Courtesy of Gary and Niki Giberson.*

Chapter 16

"The Stump Jumper Who Made a Million"

T hey were always together, you can't fault that. Every function, every award, every specialness in their life," Sandy Costa, Ethel's niece, said.

Fred was lost without Ethel. He was paralyzed to the point of not functioning when she passed out at home. He was hospitalized when she was hospitalized. He was in shock and drugged at her funeral. Like a ship thrown off course by an unexpected storm, he struggled to navigate uncertain new waters.

Fred had no immediate family, and his relationship with Ethel's family was strained. The Lingelbachs never understood why Ethel married Fred in the first place. And as often happens after the death of a wealthy family member, antagonism and greed emerged.

Maybe the Lingelbachs shouldn't have been surprised at what happened, because Ethel had let them down before. Bertha had worked hard for many years to help Ethel and Fred become successful. She never had a husband or family of her own. Despite her talent and industry at the Old Village in furnishing and arranging the interiors of many of the historic buildings, when the Ram's Head Inn opened, she was again relegated to the coatroom.

Lois and her husband, Bob Muller, had rearranged their lives several times because Ethel had enticed them to work for the family business with generous promises that never materialized. Ethel rewrote her will again and again in attempts to ensure the Mullers' complete dedication to her projects. The Noyeses' attorney, Herbert Rothenberg, told Lois, "I can't tell you how many wills I have made for Ethel."

The Mullers' daughters were also an important part of the family business. Christine, the elder daughter, was bright and industrious and worked by Ethel's side for many years. When she was just eight years old, she helped check coats at Quail Hill on weekends. By the time she was twelve, she was a hostess. Mae Carrow said, "Christine Muller was a dead ringer for Ethel Noyes, and just as sharp. If those three, Ethel, Chris and Sandy Costa [Ev's daughter] were a team, there would be no end to what they could do. They were just inspirational people to be around."

Niki Giberson agreed. "Chris was groomed to be Ethel. She thought she was going to move into the Ram's Head Inn and be the person who took over. So it was difficult."

The younger Muller daughter, Terri, was also a hostess at Smithville. Terri was not of the same mold as her sister but enterprising in her own right. Ethel's father, Chris, had moved to Riverside Drive in Port Republic when he remarried. He raised vegetables there. Terri set up a strategically placed stand near the Inn and the General Store and sold her grandfather's produce.

With this background of promises and unmet expectations, it is not surprising that family feuds erupted shortly after the funeral. Ethel's family thought that in the end their devotion, hard work and sacrifice would be rewarded. This was not the case, however. No matter how many wills Ethel may have written, the one that stood was filed on February 7, 1973, at the Atlantic County Surrogate's office. It was signed by Ethel and witnessed by Herbert Rothenberg and Carl Fiore. Ethel bequeathed all the personal and household effects she owned at the time of her death to her beloved husband, Fred W. Noyes, if he survived her. She also bequeathed "outright in fee simple absolute to my beloved husband, Fred W. Noyes, a sum equal to one-half of the total of my gross estate." The remainder of the estate was bequeathed to the Mr. and Mrs. Fred Winslow Noyes Historical and Cultural Foundation, a New Jersey Charitable Corporation.

The seventh provision of the will states, "If my husband, Fred W. Noyes, predeceases me, I give, devise and bequeath my entire estate" as follows: $5,000 each to Bertha Lingelbach, Harry Lingelbach, Everett Lingelbach, Terry Muller, Christine Muller and Lois Muller. All the rest was given to the Mr. and Mrs. Fred Winslow Noyes Historical and Cultural Foundation. Fred W. Noyes, Herbert Rothenberg, Esquire and Carl Fiore, CPA were named coexecutors.

The Lingelbach family had been essentially left out of the will. They thought Ethel meant to leave her sisters, at least, a tangible token of her appreciation. Bertha especially was incredulous. She believed Ethel intended her to have some of the beautiful antiques they both cherished. As the Lingelbachs pressed their case, Lois said Fred began to refer to them as "the goddamned family."

Niki Giberson said, "There was no love lost between Bert and Fred. She was there taking care of him after Ethel died because she loved her sister. Bert lived there a long time. And she hated him; I mean she really hated him. Fred wasn't very nice to her, but she was the kind of person to put up with a lot. She was kind of protecting Ethel's stuff. She would sleep there and leave every morning to go do her business, go to her house. She slept in the meekest quarters of the whole place, the servants' quarters. If I could describe her, she mother-henned Ethel's possessions, she loved them so much. She had the same love for artifacts that Ethel had."

Bert hoped some of the antiques would come her way. She said, "There was a painting of Ethel. Fred was going to throw it out! It was done right after they got married. She didn't like it; it didn't look like her. But when he said he was going to throw it out, I said I would take it. I'm surprised that he didn't charge me $100 for it." Eventually, Bertha found several bags of heirlooms and mementos on her front porch. There was no more to be done.

Fred had a style of his own, and it did not include looking back. His life partner and companion was gone. He missed Ethel, but he always chose his own friends, and they did not include the family.

One of the first problems facing Fred was what to do with the Ram's Head Inn. His public stance was reported in an article in the *Press of Atlantic City* just two weeks after Ethel's death: "Noyes' Inn Won't Shut, Not for Sale." "We had an extraordinarily large number of telephone calls from out of town to determine whether we would continue operation," said an inn staff member. Reports of the restaurant's closing or sale were especially widespread in the Philadelphia and New York areas where the inn had a large following. Fred quashed these rumors and stated, "In her honor and in her memory, the Ram's Head Inn will continue to operate in the traditionally elegant manner that was Mrs. Noyes' hallmark."

Creating and operating a first-class restaurant may have suited Ethel, but it was not how Fred wanted spend his time. He wanted to paint and to document and catalogue his decoy collection. He wanted to enjoy life on his terms with his friends. It didn't take long for this to happen.

On October 31, 1979, attorney Herbert Rothenberg announced an agreement of sale for the Ram's Head Inn for an undisclosed amount. The successful buyers were Harry and Doris Knowles, who, along with their sons, were operators of the Manor, a posh and expansive restaurant in West Orange, New Jersey. The deal was expected to close within thirty to sixty days, according to Rothenberg.

"The role of the Noyes family under the new owners is undecided, but Mr. Noyes plans to devote a substantial amount of time to the Noyes Foundation," said Rothenberg. The foundation was involved in planning a folklore museum that would document the historic, cultural and economic development of South Jersey. Several sites for the museum were under consideration at the time.

Now Fred was free to pursue his plans, and he wanted the Gibersons with him. Niki remembered, "In February, right after Ethel died, we started working for Fred on Gary's days off, on Mondays and Tuesdays. We would go down and work on the decoys. We would help with the meals. It gave the other people who were helping Fred a break, and they could leave on those days. If he needed to be driven somewhere, whatever he wanted, we just kept him company. We really liked Fred; we liked being part of someone's dream like that. On April 1, April Fools day of 1979, we started working for him full time, from eight in the morning until eight at night, seven days a week. There was so much work that needed to be done to catalogue the decoy collection.

"We started cataloging his decoy collection," continued Niki. "He had 3,500 decoys; some were in the basement, some were in the attic. Sometimes the head was in the basement and the body was in the outbuilding. We put all these decoys together and took eight-by-ten photographs of each one. I would hold the decoy on my lap, and Fred would punch numbers in them so each decoy was numbered. We had an information sheet on each decoy showing who it came from, who made it, what kind of paint it had, what kind of undercoat, how big the lead weight was. I mean, everything about this decoy was in this cataloguing system. While we would be sitting there, Fred would tell me stories about Ethel and he, how they originally had an antique shop and so on.

"Fred said Ethel's whole goal was to be a millionaire. As soon as she made her first million, she said, 'You know Fred, there ain't much to a million.' And he said, 'Well, you better keep going.' She would say, 'You know, I have this really great idea, but I'm going to have to go a million in debt to do it.' And he would say, 'Oh what the hell, go ahead and do it.'"

Fred's reminiscing was a needed catharsis. He talked at length about the two people he loved and missed, Ethel and his father. Fred's artistic talent began with his father, and Ethel encouraged it. "He spoke a lot about his father," said Niki, "not as much about his mother. I know he idolized his father. Fred was very, very lonely. His whole purpose in life was gone when Ethel died. She was the driving force."

The Gibersons helped fill the gap in Fred's life. Cataloguing the decoy collection was the overt reason to have them there everyday, but Fred admitted, "Gary, you know if you weren't working for me, I wouldn't even do this. But I want you around, and I don't know what else to do with you." Gary added, "I wasn't there for the money, I was there to help him. I'll tell you how close I was to Fred Noyes; I used to cut his toenails. That is something I would do for my father."

Fred continued to expand his decoy collection. Some dealers regarded him as an easygoing, wealthy widower, an easy target for an inflated sale.

"I saw people take advantage of him," said Gary. "There was an art dealer who was trying to sell him some fakes, a pair of bogus mergansers. I knew it. I was wondering what I could do because Fred was talking very friendly with this guy. I get this terrible migraine headache, and I'm saying to myself, 'Fred, how can you do this; no, no, no.' I told him the next day, 'Fred, you got stung yesterday. I'm your advisor and your buyer. We need a communication system. When I scratch my elbow, that means, Fred buy this, this is excellent.' Then I said, 'Fred, you have to give me signals, when I can buy more and when to stop.' So he said, 'Okay. If I rub my head that means go higher; if I touch my collar that means cut off.' So now we can be in front of dealers, and we can communicate. He loved it! We really had fun.

"See, I knew his checkbook," Gary continued. We would buy $7,000 to $8,000 worth of decoys at a time. Fred Noyes was what they call a heavy hitter, the number one buyer. We've got dealers coming out of Texas, sending us their decoys. We bought the best decoys. Other buyers are mad because we are paying high prices, but we are getting really good birds, award pieces.

"He had a pilot, Wayne Kiser, and we are flying in the Cessna 411 to see some of these birds. Unbelievable what I'm involved with, spending his money for something I love. He really didn't need more, he already had 3,500."

Fred loved to have company for lunch. A valued guest was fellow artist Paul Stankard. By this time, Stankard was on his way to becoming "the greatest living master of the paperweight maker's art in the world." Four or five times a year, Paul drove from his home in Mantua in southwest New Jersey to visit Fred.

Chef and sometime chauffeur Earl Robinson drove Fred and Paul on the Garden State Parkway and in the Forsythe Wildlife Preserve.

Stankard commented, "Even in the dead of winter, Fred pointed out, 'How beautiful—see the greens, the cedar, the holly, the view of the bay and the ocean.' Fred loved the land so much and saw such beauty in it. He made me want to move there."

Fred supported Paul by purchasing more than fifty of his paperweights at wholesale prices. Paul bought his first Cadillac not long after meeting Fred. Part-time housekeeper Barbara McLaughlin recalled the paperweight collection. "Fred had a gorgeous collection of paperweights. I think they were supposed to go to the museum. I wasn't allowed to clean in the room with the paperweights, I wasn't allowed to dust or anything. He used to yell at me, 'You get out of that room, little girl.'

"Fred's closest companion was a white Scottish terrier named Lee Mackey who would lie by him when he painted in the sunroom or sit on his lap when he had company," Barbara said. "There was always a lot of dog hair."

Without Ethel there to structure his day, Fred was free to do what he liked. On a whim, he would fly to Maryland for a plate of crab cakes.

Gary Giberson captured the *joie de vivre* when he related, "This was really an exciting part of my life that went by too quickly. 'We are taking a day off!' Fred would say, 'Call Wayne!' That was the pilot, Wayne Kiser. Marty Holderson was co-pilot. That plane couldn't take off unless it had a pilot and a co-pilot because it was a two-engine plane, a six or eight-seater. This is how wealthy people do things. It was like flying around the country with John D. Rockefeller. The plane wouldn't take off unless there were fresh bottles in a little velvet bag. Fred had Crown Royal. I had Chivas Regal. It is like drinking something from the King and Queen of Scotland. They were beautiful wonderful days.

"I had never been to the Statue of Liberty, and Fred flew me around it three times. I remember he said, 'Take him around again, Wayne!' He would bank the plane, and I could look right down. It is a wonder the park service didn't fire a gun! You couldn't do that today."

In the spring of 1981, the *Press of Atlantic City* reporter Ed Hitzel visited Fred in Port Republic. Ed's father was in the hotel business, and he and Fred had mutual friends. Ed wondered how Fred was managing now that Ethel was gone.

"Well, I called him and he said, 'Come have lunch.' I didn't know whether he meant we would sit down and have a cheeseburger or what. It turned out to be a formal lunch. It was quite an experience. He wasn't pretentious at all, right down to earth, no bullshit. He and I got along well. I felt like I was in the presence of a family member, like an uncle. We could talk about anything. It was like an exchange between two people with common interests instead of a reporter and a subject."

The result of the interview was "The Stump Jumper Who Made a Million," printed in the *Press of Atlantic City* on Sunday April 12, 1981. A "stump jumper" was someone who lived a few miles inland and trapped and fished.

"I'm a pain in the rear end, actually," said Fred, "Ethel says that anyway, my wife used to say." Hitzel wrote that in spite of the Noyeses' impressive business achievements, Fred maintained an earthy attitude toward pomp and circumstance. He didn't like "monkey suits" and sometimes dressed casually even for formal affairs. "In the area social and business community, Fred Noyes is legend, and people treat him like a precious metal no matter how he is dressed."

"You know," said Niki Giberson, "Fred liked to do things for the shock appeal. He was very outspoken, and it didn't matter to him. He loved watching people and their reactions. He would do or say something and sit back and watch the action happen. He loved to come out of the kitchen at the Ram's Head Inn with a shrimp in between each one of his fingers and say, 'Here, want to try one?'"

Fred also got a kick out of playing the women in his life against each other and watching the sparks fly. One woman Fred was interested in was the attractive housekeeper, Marge Glass. "He wanted to buy Marge a house," said Barbara McLaughlin, "but she didn't want a relationship with him. She just wanted to be a professional caretaker. She would say, 'No, you're not going to do that,' or 'No, I'm not cooking that for you.'" If it came to vying for Fred's attention, Marge preferred to bow out.

Not one to bow out was Eleanor Miller, notorious bookkeeper at the Ram's Head Inn whose relationship with Fred had caused Ethel so much distress. Brash and hotheaded, Eleanor was a good subject for gossip. Florence Miller, Ethel's friend from the Atlantic County Cultural and Heritage Advisory Board, said Eleanor cleared out all Ethel's clothes on the very day of her funeral.

When the Knowleses took over the Rams Head Inn, they fired Eleanor. She went to work for Fred as his bookkeeper, but she wanted to be more than that. Eleanor loved to cook, and that certainly endeared her to Fred. Niki Giberson said, "Fred bought her a house in Smithville and had the whole thing decorated by Kensingston, the top local furniture store. The décor was sparkly wallpaper and red plush carpeting. That was his little getaway."

Ed Hitzel used to see Fred and Eleanor at the Point Pub in Somers Point. "The Point Pub was one of the premier restaurants in the county then, and a lot of businessmen and politicians went there. I would see him out all the time with Eleanor, whom I assumed was his girlfriend. That is what he said too. She was very nice. I remember her being a big blond woman, gregarious, very friendly, certainly enjoyed a good meal, as did he. Fred had the reputation for enjoying women. It occurred to me that it is a good thing that he wasn't born later, because with all the sexual harassment issues today, Smithville would have been owned by some eighteen-year-old waitress. I mean, I saw him grabbing people. He never quit. Eleanor had a sense of humor about it. She was very nicely dressed; you could tell she was used to going out to nice places. He had a cane or walker at that point; he was having a hard time."

The other woman on the scene was longtime acquaintance and real estate agent Helene Walls. Helene was arguably worldlier than Eleanor, having spent time abroad, and she came across to Stankard as a "kinder soul." Helene had a beautiful face with high cheekbones, lively eyes and a sophisticated carriage. Fred's attraction to Helene was clear. Stankard remembered sitting on the porch with Fred and Helene. "Fred looked at me in a stern way and said, 'It's time for you to go.'"

Jack Lamping's remembers difficulties around the women. "Eleanor Miller was a German woman, very efficient. She had maps made of all the properties and their various uses. When Ethel died, she took Fred over. She used some of the funds for herself and her family. She would dominate Fred. He was easily dominated at this point. She got him to Florida; he became her prisoner down there. He had no way of getting back. She bought cars and homes for her son from company funds. There was a local woman who was mindful of his needs who helped rescue him, Helene."

A vivid picture of Fred's personal life at this time is revealed in the photographs from his seventy-sixth birthday party on April 22, 1981, at Quail Hill. One would not guess that two of the women who figured prominently in the photographs were at war over Fred. The birthday party was a temporary truce between Eleanor Miller and Helene Walls as they vied for first place in Fred's life. And it was evident that Fred enjoyed every minute of being the center of all this attention. The story is that Fred agreed to let Eleanor give him the party and have all the glory for putting that together if Helene would be invited and sit at Fred's right. The party invitation read "A Great Party for a Great Guy and Gentleman." The guests included many prominent Atlantic County residents, family and friends, all of whom temporarily ignored any troubles that may have existed among them. If the Lingelbachs were angry with Fred, the smiling faces of Bertha Lingelbach, her sister Lois and Lois's husband, Bob Muller, belied any bad feelings. Architect Paul Cope and his wife and Gary and Niki Giberson were there.

At Fred's table, in addition to Helene, were the two foundation trustees, Carl Fiore and Herbert Rothenberg, and their wives and Betsy and John Rogge.

In the photographs, Helene, radiant in a pale pink décolleté knit, poses happily with her arm around Fred's shoulders. Eleanor, in an equally chummy pose, leans from behind against a seated Fred, one hand over his shoulder and planted firmly on his chest as if to prevent him from moving away from her. With her other hand, she presents him with a large signed birthday card from the group. Eleanor was dressed severely in a high-necked black dress with a white collar and black satin bow; her blond hair was shellacked in a high twist and pulled back tightly from her face. The prim presentation, so unlike her personality, seems a grim effort to imitate Ethel. In another photo, Eleanor has wedged herself between Helene and Fred, her hands on Fred's shoulders, when Fred was presented with his four-tiered birthday cake. Helene, laughing and clapping her hands, appears relaxed and Eleanor overly eager. Fred is in his glory.

The dinner was surely chosen to please Fred's simple and robust taste and Eleanor's German heritage: roast loin of pork, sauerkraut, broiled flounder, mashed and baked potatoes and apple crisp for dessert. The evening closed with a musical program from a group that Fred enjoyed, the Young at Heart.

Many people close to Fred shared this significant evening. Fred was buoyant with love and attention surrounding him. But before long, many of these seemingly happy relationships would be cracked and shattered.

Both Eleanor and Helene had strong personalities, and the situation could not last. Eleanor was tempestuous and erratic. Helene's strength lay in her ability to keep cool and play for the long term.

"The final straw was when Fred took Helene out to lunch. Eleanor didn't want him to, and he did anyway. So she came over to the house while he was gone. She went into the kitchen and took all the dishes out of the cabinet and threw them all the way down, towards the porch. She was so mad at him," said Niki Giberson.

The game was over. Fred dimissed Eleanor from his service and from his life.

Chapter 17

THE LEGACY BECOMES REALITY

No matter what else was going on, Fred pursued his dream to build a museum in Ethel's memory. She had been passionate about preserving South Jersey history, and a museum would enshrine that passion. The area would have something it never had before—a place where adults and children could learn about the past. The museum would also promote contemporary regional artists.

"The Noyeses took quite a few artists under their wing," recalled Niki Giberson. "They felt it was their job to help these artists make a living so they could continue their work. There was a man named Jay Parker. The most famous things he made were these roosters, these silly looking whimsical roosters. Fred bought every single one he ever made. Parker would say, 'Well you gave me six bucks for the last one, I've got to get seven for this one.' Fred would say, 'Alright.'"

Instead of Ethel as his partner in planning the museum, Fred now had the foundation. In her will, Ethel appointed Fred W. Noyes, Herbert Rothenberg and Carl Fiore as executors. She designated the same three as trustees of the Mr. and Mrs. Fred Winslow Noyes Historical and Cultural Foundation. Consequently, Fred had only one third of the voting power. In such a triumvirate, two opposing opinions would be decided by the third vote. The strongest member of a triumvirate need only persuade one of the other two to win his point of view. The dynamic of the personalities in this powerful group was crucial to the direction taken by the foundation and, ultimately, to the outcome of the museum.

Fred liked to come off as a country bumpkin, but he was not stupid, said Rothenberg's partner Michael Hyett. "Fred was playing a role, Country Boy. He was always joking and good old boy stuff. But he was very knowledgeable about the history of the region."

But he was no match for the brilliant Herbert Rothenberg. Senior partner in the law firm of Rothenberg, Hyett and Eisen in Atlantic City, Rothenberg held a bachelor of science degree from the Wharton School of Business at the University of Pennsylvania, a law degree from Yale and a Master of Laws in Taxation from New York University. A first lieutenant in the U.S. Air Force, Office of Special Investigation, Rothenberg also served on the Office of Chief Counsel for the Internal Revenue Service. He was on the boards of three foundations. He had a forceful personality and could be intimidating.

When the IRS audited Smithville in the late 1960s and claimed Smithville owed $500,000 in taxes, Carl Fiore brought in Herb Rothenberg as tax attorney. Rothenberg turned things around so that Smithville got a $100,000 refund. Duly impressed, Ethel started going to him for advice. Carl said Rothenberg was "like a personal attorney for Ethel." He became special counsel on the board of directors of Smithville, Inc. (Kirkman, who was general counsel for the Noyeses, had wanted to take over and became jealous of the influence Rothenberg had with Ethel.)

Rothenberg guided the Noyeses through the public offering of 1972, the sale of Smithville in 1974, the purchase of the Dutch Barn and the establishment of the foundation. This long-term familiarity and knowledge of their affairs gave him power. He influenced many aspects of their lives, including recommending investments. He observed how Fred and Ethel worked together over the years and formed his opinion about their relationship.

Rothenberg lived in Margate, a markedly different community from Port Republic. Margate residents tended to be wealthier and better educated, and more were in professional occupations. A number were summer residents who lived and earned their living in Philadelphia. Herb traveled in cosmopolitan circles. Fred, on the other hand, would rather mess with his paints or go fishing than attend a stuffy board meeting. Fred didn't even have a high school diploma. And he was more vulnerable without Ethel. Rothenberg's attitude toward him became one of disdain.

"Rothenberg took the foundation over and used it for his own," observed attorney Don Phillips. "He replaced Kirkman as Ethel's attorney for tax purposes. He was a 'smoothie.' I remember when he came to town. He was in the Schwinn Building. Rothenberg was working on Ethel to seduce her to come with him because he wanted to build a mighty law firm." Other professional peers had even less flattering opinions of Rothenberg.

The third member of the triumvirate, Carl Fiore, respected Rothenberg and admired the way he structured Ethel's will. "When she died, it was set up so half would go to Fred, because half could escape taxation. The other half went to the Noyes Foundation, which was tax free, so there was practically no tax when she died."

Carl was mild-mannered, reliable, straightforward and sensitive. Fiore and Rothenberg had regarded Ethel as their peer, while Fred remained on the periphery. Now Fred, the widower, the artist, the "stump jumper" got lucky, was thrust to the foreground. He was the odd man out in the triumvirate.

The original Noyes Foundation (#1), established in 1965 to offer college scholarships to high school graduates, was composed of personal friends and associates of the Noyeses. They included New Jersey author and historian John Cunningham; Ocean County Freeholder director Jack Lamping; Dr. Peter Sammartino of Fairleigh-Dickinson University; Mary Roebling, head of Trenton Trust Company; Elwood Kirkman; George Keppel; and accountant Robert Lunny.

Semiannually, the student screening committee presented applicants for approval. Then the meetings evolved into a discussion of some project Ethel was working on. She used the group as her sounding board. "The foundation didn't really do very much, and it was totally subservient to her will. It was always a discussion of her ideas," said Lamping.

John Cunningham said, "Take a look at that list of people. She was able to convince all of us that it would be to our benefit to be on this foundation."

A second foundation, the Mr. and Mrs. Fred Winslow Noyes Historical and Cultural Foundation (#2), a New Jersey Charitable Corporation Foundation, was cited in Ethel's will of February 7, 1973, and was the beneficiary of half of her estate. Information required to be published about the foundation was posted in the *Jewish Record* and it became an operating foundation on January 15, 1974.

The original Noyes Foundation (#1) was abruptly disbanded shortly after Ethel's death. On July 30, 1979, the board of trustees of the second foundation (#2) sent a letter to the members of the original foundation (#1) advising them it had been decided to terminate their funding. The second foundation (#2) would instead direct its immediate charitable contributions to support the expansion of the Atlantic City Medical Center Foundation. They (#2) had recently pledged $50,000 to the hospital's building campaign. The letter stated, "The basic thrust of the Mr. and Mrs. Fred Winslow Noyes Foundation is the creation of the Fred and Ethel Noyes Folklore Museum. This project is now beginning to take shape, and we feel it will constitute a lasting memorial to Ethel Noyes."

Why did the Atlantic City Medical Center suddenly become a beneficiary of the new foundation? Ethel had been on the board of the medical center, and she had died there. More significantly, Herbert Rothenberg was the president of the board of trustees of the medical center.

The members of the original Noyes Foundation (#1) were surprised and hurt by the abrupt termination. Jack Lamping said, "The foundation was taken over by Rothenberg, an ambitious lawyer. All of us were dismissed. We were no longer invited to any of the meetings."

Significantly, the first signature on the letter was Herbert Rothenberg's. Fred's signature was underneath and Carl Fiore's beneath that. The pecking order was established.

The first task of the new foundation was to find an architect for the museum project. The foundation chose Cope and Lippincott Architects from Philadelphia. Paul Cope had an Atlantic City connection. His widowed father married Mae Bell after Ezra died. Paul recalled, "I really got started early. When we went to the different hotels in Atlantic City, I would draw on the back of menus."

The next task was to find the site for the museum. The first choice was a site on the Nacote Creek in Port Republic that Fred owned. The old Bowen house, full of stored antiques, stood on the site, but there was ground for a museum and parking.

Trouble was brewing in Port Republic, however.

The plans for the museum were presented at the monthly zoning board meeting. City hall was packed, and there was standing room only. Over 80 of the 750 residents showed up. Fred sat in the front row with Herbert Rothenberg, Paul Cope and Gary Giberson. After Rothenberg made a case for the advantages of the museum and Cope explained his architectural plan, the citizenry was invited to speak. One by one, residents got up and expressed their fears of unwanted traffic, busloads of gawking tourists and trash that would disrupt their town's tranquility. Fred leaned over and whispered to Rothenberg, who stood and asked for a break. A few minutes later, Rothenberg returned alone. He said that due to the number and sincere nature of the objections to the proposed museum, Mr. Noyes was withdrawing his application.

Later, Fred confided to Gary Giberson, "If there is one person who is not in favor of me building this museum here, I will go somewhere else. I don't want people throwing stones at the thing."

Paul Cope had a more dramatic recollection. "The public raised all these terrible visions of South Philadelphia mobs coming in and throwing beer cans all over and the parking and pollution and all the terrible things that were going to happen there if we built a museum in the little village. Fred just backed off and said the hell with this; it's not worth fighting. Fred liked the idea of doing it in Port Republic. It was his stomping ground. But he wasn't going to waste a lot of time and money and heartache fighting it, and there were other opportunities."

Indeed, other opportunities were just around the corner. Stockton State College wanted the museum, but with the stipulation that a certain number of professors be on the board of directors. Fred declined the offer.

Next Fred started looking in Galloway Township. The chauffeur couldn't drive one day, so Gary drove. They went to Lily Lake and drove along the north side, where the cabin used for entertaining soldiers during World War II had been. Across the lake was a Boy Scout camp called Little Indian Day Camp. Part of the property was cleared and opened down an incline to the water's edge. Fred was struck by the location and decided on the spot that this was where he wanted the museum.

As Gary tells it, "Fred went up and knocked on the door and said, 'I want to buy this property.' And the guy said, 'Well, it's really not for sale.' Fred says, 'How many acres you got?' 'There's three here and five across the road.' 'I'll give you a quarter of a million for it.' The guy looked over Fred's shoulder and saw the limousine and said, 'You're serious aren't you?' Fred said, 'You're damn right I'm serious. I want to build my museum here.' The guy said, 'You what?' Fred said, 'An art museum, a decoy museum. When can your lawyer meet my lawyer? How about this afternoon?' The guy said, 'How about tomorrow?' So that is how we bought the property."

Helene Walls had another version of the acquisition. "After Ethel died, I was called in to find a site for the museum. I found the Little Indian Day Camp. It was listed. It worked extremely well."

In any case, Fred was thrilled with the eight-acre property in a wooded setting that included a water view. The site was a half mile off the main highway and next to the Brigantine National Wildlife Refuge, now the Edwin B. Forsythe National Wildlife Refuge. The preserve stretched east to Great Bay and was host to ducks, geese, shorebirds and other wildlife of the wetlands that Fred loved so much.

Architect Paul Cope was equally enthusiastic about the site. When he first saw the property with its thirty-five-foot drop to the lake, he knew immediately how the museum would be laid out. He called the design site specific, because he let the topography of the site dictate the plan of the building. He told Gary Giberson, 'I'll build this museum right down the hill.' Cope envisioned the visitor to the museum would see just what he saw that day, a riveting view between the trees down to the lake and water lilies.

Plans for the museum proceeded. Cope commented, "Fred didn't come to the job meetings. He was laid-back. He didn't intrude in the whole process; Gary spoke for him." Gary had significant input as the concept and design developed over the coming months. He recommended both the siding and flooring materials, which were native to South Jersey. The exterior was white cedar stained a weathered grey. The flooring was end-grain fir and was a work of art in itself. Yellow pine was used for the woodwork and baseboards. All the millwork was finely turned by John Clark of Pleasantville.

The architect strove to combine the old and the new. Cedar siding, weathered wood shingles on the roof and exposed interior framing timbers were reminiscent of classic barn construction. At the same time, the sharply angled roof lines, the skylights, the generous windows and spacious floor areas were clean and stunningly contemporary. The museum was built to be energy efficient. The high glass panels facing south were passive solar collectors, using the sun to both light and heat the building.

Cope added, "The museum was done using natural light, but the light doesn't directly hit the artwork. There are baffles to shield the light from the south, and the skylights on the roof all face north. We tried to do some passive solar heating by putting fans up by the glass panels so the heat is circulated downward."

The layout achieved the architect's initial vision. Upon entering, visitors immediately experienced a breathtaking view down the multileveled central gallery through a wall of glass to Lily Lake. Four gallery wings perpendicular to the central gallery alternated, two on each side, down the levels toward the lake. Between the gallery wings were landscaped courts seen through the glass walls of the central gallery.

Perfect, but not quite so perfect from another point of view. Gary noted: "Well, when you build something down a hill, you got steps. You walk down to one wing, and you walk down to another wing. I liked it when he first designed it, but after you work in it and have to go up and down and move art up and down, well…" Also, the levels proved a challenge for the handicapped. Anyone in a wheelchair must go outside to get from one level to another.

Fortunately, Paul Cope and Gary Giberson thought alike. Their work relationship began from the moment the site was cleared until the museum was completed one and a half years later. Cope's business was in Philadelphia, but Gary could be on site every day to monitor construction.

Gary said, "The builder was M.B. Markland, who did a fabulous job, and the foreman for the job was John Mong. He was excellent; he had worked for them for years. I got along so well with them and with all the Union contractors. Jenkins did the plumbing, Burrows the electric.

"After it was all done, Paul wrote me the most beautiful letter. Problems happen, and you have to change this or that and they usually allow 10 to 15 percent for changes. I think there was one change to Paul's design, a heating duct, and that was the only change order on the whole job. Paul said he had never worked on a job that had less than 2 percent change orders. He thanked me so much for that; I was sort of his agent on the job. The final cost was $1,507,577."

In addition to 9,000 square feet of gallery and circulation area, there was 1,500 square feet designated for administration and support functions. A 1,000-square-foot fireproof vault was built in the basement to house and safely preserve the decoy collection. And there was a receiving area with a loading dock.

Gary cared passionately that the museum be built to high standards and according to plan. His money was not at stake, but his values were. He had idolized Ethel Noyes. There would be no compromising on the museum being built in her honor.

"One time one of the brick layers was drunk and didn't use corner blocks on the front of the museum. I brought it to his attention, and he said, 'Shut up now, I can't do nothing about it, I run out of corner blocks.' I went over to the pile, and it was full of corner blocks. Then he made the excuse he didn't see them. He was just lazy. I waited until they all went home. Then I kicked three courses off the wall because I wanted the building done right. No one ever knew that, I'm confessing here. If I had told Fred, he would have said good for you!"

Paul Cope added, "Gary spotted the fact that some of the lumber was not up to snuff. We were well into construction by then and modified the design a bit, thanks to his eagle eye."

Paul also noted the beginning of dissension. "Gary was a great asset; he had a good eye for the wood, being a carver. He was very oriented toward carving and the ducks and so forth. Herb Rothenberg was interested in the fine arts aspect of the museum. So there were slightly different visions, and the museum had to accommodate both ideas."

Paul remembered dealing with Fred only sporadically. It was Cope's impression right from the beginning that Rothenberg was determined to be in charge. Fred brought Gary with him to the foundation meetings.

Giberson said, "Well, the first time I walked in the room, Rothenberg said to Fred, 'Does Giberson have to be here?' Fred told him, 'Every time I come to this building, Gary will be with me and Gary will sit on my right side. Gary will be in every meeting we have, and Gary will be involved in every decision that is made at this table.' He said it emphatically. It was one of the most emphatic statements I have ever heard Fred Noyes say."

As the museum progressed, so did the discord among the trustees. The issue was not about money. There seemed to be plenty of that. Paul Cope affirmed that the financial aspect of working on the museum was a pleasure. Bills were paid on time, and the project budget was ample. "The final cost was a million and a half, $1,507,577. The cost was a little more than expected, there were $28,577 in change orders. But there were no money hassles."

Control of the foundation dollars and how those dollars would be spent was at stake. Fred knew what he wanted, and so did Rothenberg. The balance of power would have tipped in a different direction if Ethel had been one of the players.

"I watched Fred be disheartened," said Gary. "I would go to business meetings, and I would see it. Then I would go out to the car with Fred, and Fred would cry all the way home to Port Republic, just sit there with tears coming out of his eyes. I would say, 'What is the matter, Fred?' He would just shake his head.

"You know what Rothenberg's favorite expression was? 'Ha, ha, ha, Fred…NO, you can't do that.' If I heard him say that once, I heard him say it a thousand times. Things like "Okay, Fred, we will try to. We will try to work that in. Ha, ha, ha, Fred…NO, you can't do that.'"

It was the very character and mission of the museum that was under dispute. Paul Cope said, "Oh, I had forgotten the phrase. It was a 'Folk Art Museum,' that was how they kept referring to it in the beginning.

"Fred, of course, had his duck decoy collection which he wanted to house and protect and display. He also had this collection of primitive Americana he wanted to display. And at that time, there was no real fine arts museum in South Jersey. So that seemed like a great thing for the foundation to do."

When the foundation expanded the purpose to include the fine arts, "Folk Art" was dropped from the name of the museum.

The decoy collection was given priority. The largest gallery, located on the right, one level down from the entrance, was designed to display the decoys on a rotating basis in the first section of the room. The rest of the gallery was devoted to Gary Giberson and his woodworking shop, where he demonstrated carving and told tales of the South Jersey pines. Gary's office was behind the work area. This gallery successfully carried through on Ethel's idea for the Old Village at Smithville, demonstrating historic objects along with an artist at work.

Gary said, "Fred wanted the decoys shown as art. Not as folk art or anything like that. He said, 'I want them at eye level. I don't want any cases to look like shoe cases, we are not going to have a shoe store.'"

Initially, Cope worked on the plans for the decoy display, but the project was determined important enough to bring in an installation specialist. Richard Conway Meyer, a Philadelphia architect whose work included an installation at the Philadelphia Museum of Art, was hired. A fireproof vault was built in the basement to protect the collection that was worth millions.

Cope emphasized, "I designed the building as a general art museum that could display artwork of any kind, not just ducks. The other three galleries were neutral. You know, any kind of art could be displayed."

Each gallery was composed of ten-foot modules. The largest gallery, where Gary had his workshop and office, had six ten-foot modules. The next two galleries each had five modules. The fourth gallery on the lowest level on the right was originally intended for Fred and the artists he wanted to exhibit.

Fred planned to paint and have an office there. But the gallery design was modified to have only four modules, no studio or office. It was just the beginning of a number of decisions that disheartened him.

"You know, they wouldn't allow Fred to have an office. There is still a phone jack there where he was to have his own private line. He would be set up to do his own private painting," said Gary. "They wouldn't allow him to paint in the building. I could work there, but Fred couldn't. That broke his heart."

Next came the search for a director. This individual would have the opportunity to mold the museum literally from the ground up. The challenge would be to attract visitors to an out-of-the way rural location. Among those seeking the job was an impressive candidate, Anne Fabbri, director of the Deshong Museum at Widener University and a well-known art historian and writer. She had a degree from Radcliffe and a master of arts from Bryn Mawr College and had studied at the University of Venice.

Anne recalled, "I saw the ad in the 'Career Opportunity' publication by the AAM, the American Association of Museums. They were looking for a founding director for this new museum of contemporary art. They wanted someone who was knowledgeable in contemporary art and would do rotating exhibitions of national and international art, including New Jersey artists."

This was quite a change from a Folk Art Museum featuring local art, historic objects, decoys and demonstrating artists.

The trustees offered her the job in the summer of 1982 while the museum was still under construction. Anne said, "The walls were up when I started. The interior walls were up, and the skylights were in. But the skylights had to have ultraviolet filters, and no one had thought of that. So I told them. Also all the windows in the hallway."

Paul Cope said he wished Anne had come on board earlier in the process. Anne agreed, "Then he and I could have worked together on certain things. He said it was difficult because he had no one to consult with about the basic needs, where the janitorial closet would be, the storage for the rotating exhibits when one came down and another went up, a library and so forth.

"The foundation offered me an apartment down in the area. But I felt I had to be connected to Center City for everything, for public relations, for networking. Especially when starting a new museum. I was excited about the opportunity. It was the first art museum in southern New Jersey. I told them as soon as we have done a couple of shows, we can apply for grants from the state. They had not thought of that. So this expanded the opportunity."

Working at the Noyes Museum meant Fabbri had to drive an hour and a half from her home in Olde City, Philadelphia. But she was exhilarated by the chance to start from scratch. She made all decisions, from what stationery and logo to use to major policies determining whose work to exhibit and collect. Carl Fiore said, "She was reminiscent of Ethel. She was a mover. She got things done, and she didn't antagonize people."

Anne had a good relationship with the trustees and found them very supportive. She regarded Carl as a very nice man but not sophisticated in art at all. "Carl would stop in, and we would have lunch and confer over finances."

In Herb Rothenberg, she found a fellow connoisseur of art. "Herb was wonderful. He and his wife, Lois, were very interested in art. They invited me to their apartment in New York overlooking Central Park. They were collectors and had some beautiful works of art. Privately they bought a few things from exhibitions at the museum. Their apartment was near the Metropolitan Museum of Art, and they were members there. They were also members of the Museum of Modern Art, the Whitney and the Guggenheim, so they were very knowledgeable in art. Herb could see the state was interested in giving us money because we were bringing art to the southern part of New Jersey when there really was no other institution financially who could do it."

Anne's memories of Fred at this time are vague. He seemed to have been in the background, overshadowed by Herb Rothenberg.

The *Press of Atlantic City* interviewed Fabbri along with Cope and Rothenberg for a lead story on August 29, 1982. According to the reporter, it was still almost a year until opening. The museum was unfinished inside, and the collection had not been moved in. While picking her way through construction materials that littered the interior, Fabbri gave a tour of the spacious and graceful galleries, storage area and research library. She stressed the regional aspects of the museum and plans to reach out to the South Jersey community. The programs would be educational and entertaining and would utilize a collection of more than four thousand objects to its limit. The museum would be a resource for historic and scholarly pursuits as well as serve local artists.

"We wish to show contemporary artists who are currently exploring thoughts and media in innovative ways. The museum is so alive," Fabbri said. "We're a museum in transition, and our goals are multi-faceted."

Rothenberg echoed her thoughts, adding, "We want to create a museum which will be meaningful to its community."

While construction moved to completion, both Cope and Fabbri talked about growth and change in regard to the museum. Why the museum would need to change before it even opened is unclear. Interestingly, Fred was not quoted in the media at this time. He found it difficult to continually fight for what he believed the museum should be. The museum was meant to house and display the Noyeses' American folk art and decoy collection and support local artists. Fred felt the original purpose, and his ability to facilitate that purpose, was being overridden and overpowered.

The ultimate insult came when the opening event at the museum was a benefit for the Atlantic City Medical Center and not a grand opening for the museum at all. Formal invitations to the black tie dinner dance were from the "Century Club of the ACMC Foundation." The evening's elegant black-and-white program bound with a tasseled cord was titled "Celebration of the Century." Next, the Century Club and ACMC Foundation were credited. The Noyes Museum was mentioned only in small typeface at the bottom of the invitation as the location of the champagne reception. The date of the event was June 4, 1983.

There was just one photograph in the program, that of Rothenberg on the first page. His President's Message read: "This year's theme 'Celebration of the Century' relates to much more than its happy coincidence with the opening of the Noyes Museum, which we are privileged to share."

This was no coincidence. The fundraiser was staged at the Noyes Museum, but the museum certainly did not share or get even remotely equal billing at the event.

The remainder of the message and program was devoted to the medical center, its expansion, listing of committee members, trustees, board of governors and the evening's events, including an informal tour of the Noyes Galleries and the menu. The dinner dance took place in the "Grand Ballroom-in-a-Tent."

The fact that Fred and Ethel and their foundation were not mentioned spoke volumes. The fact that Gary Giberson, assistant to director Anne Fabbri, was not invited to the event and that Fred had to buy the Gibersons tickets added to the cacophony. It was as if, at the moment of completion, the museum was lifted from Fred's hands and moved out of his reach.

The fanfare of the fundraiser seemed to obscure the lack of credit given the Noyeses and their museum. Fred was a supporter of the medical center and surely put on his party face for the occasion. But so much was already lost.

After Ethel's funeral, Fred had said, "I still want to do the decoy museum. But it's got to be bigger and better than ever because it is now in Ethel's memory."

Yet during the speeches and accolades, Fred would not have been introduced had not one of the guests called out and asked the museum founder be recognized.

This gala event was not about the museum and the fact that it existed because of the vision and generosity of Fred and Ethel Noyes. Fred didn't participate in the selection of the inaugural exhibit. Little of Fred's choosing other than the decoys was there.

Without any celebration or fanfare, the museum opened to the public a week later on Sunday, June 12, 1983.

Chapter 18

ART COMES TO THE PINES

A Museum Is Built," the title of an article in the June 1983 issue of *Art Matters*, records the origin of the museum: "The idea sprang from Ethel Noyes...always in the back of her mind was the desire to build a museum for the people of South Jersey—her home—a museum that would house the unusual collection of Americana that was the particular passion of Noyes. Fred Noyes has amassed one of the largest and most comprehensive collections of duck decoys in the country. What better way to share them with the community, thought Mrs. Noyes, than to build a museum around them."

Now Ethel was gone, and new personalities took over. Anne Fabbri's interest, unlike Ethel's, was not preservation. In fact, she did not use that word at all in the museum's mission statement. Her goal was broader and more ambitious. She saw the museum as an opportunity to bring more to South Jersey than simply a memorial to its early history.

Just two weeks before the public opening in June, Fabbri spoke to a reporter at the *Press of Atlantic City*: "Actually, we are not catering to the audience. We are going to present art that is worth looking at. In other words, this is not the place to come and see a painting of a lighthouse. I'm not saying that that has no validity. That type of work, however, is wall decoration and not necessarily art...and it has no place in the context of a museum."

Referring to the opening exhibit, Fabbri said, "I think it's a conservative show. What I have been looking for, but have not found, is the artist who is doing new work. Work that is so new that it hasn't been discovered yet...new concepts, a new mode of expression. I would like to have one gallery devoted to what is new in art."

The reporter pointed out there was an element of risk involved in this bold approach. Fabbri's goal was divergent from the founders' concept of "a place where indigenous regional art forms can be preserved and studied with the heart of the museum being its large and sophisticated collection of American folk art and Fred Noyes's tremendous life time collection of hand carved hunting decoys."

Anne countered, "What I am interested in is presenting the trends in contemporary art, making this a place to come and see. For people in this area, there is no other opportunity to see art in a museum. Something I'll be very interested in is the reception of the museum on the part of the public."

The article closed with Fabbri's candid and insightful statement: "I think the museum should be an enjoyable experience for everyone in the community. I can't imagine anyone objecting to it…indifference would probably be the worst and that is probably the one thing that I will have to combat."

It wasn't long before Anne met her public. "You could really make an impact and have an effect on people's lives. I remember when we first opened, several people came in, and they said, 'What do we do now?' I said, 'Walk around and enjoy the paintings and look at the view.' I felt we were really doing something worthwhile by opening their eyes to art."

The inaugural exhibition was titled "Celebration of New Jersey Artists: From the Capital to the Cape." It was accompanied by an impressive forty-three-page glossy brochure with photographs of the artwork in which Fabbri stated, "The exhibition reveals the stylistic diversity of the visual arts now being created in New Jersey, primarily in the area extending from Trenton to Cape May." Thirty artists were represented, including David Ahlsted, Jacob Landau, Mel Leipzig and Glenn Rudderow.

Although not mentioned in the glossy brochure, Gallery II featured hundreds of decoys from Fred's collection and Gary as a carver at work. Gallery IV displayed pieces from Fred's folk art collection and some of his own work, which in its expressionist phase was found to be "quite good" by a *New York Times* reporter.

"The Question Arises: Should This Place Exist At All?" was the title of a *Philadelphia Inquirer* article that struck at the very premise of the museum. Published one month after the museum opened, the newspaper's art critic Edward Sozanski wrote, "The Noyes is, in part, a vanity museum, erected and endowed to display the art the Noyeses collected and to reflect their interest in Americana...If the inaugural Noyes material is representative of the permanent collection, then the museum will never have a parking problem, unless the transient exhibits turn out to be spectacular. Fabbri has chosen a quality show, one that I wouldn't hesitate to recommend if it were playing in Philadelphia. In terms of what it bodes for her museum, however, it left me dispirited." Sozanski commended the exhibition but questioned the museum's obscure location "proximate to the hedonist watering hole of Atlantic City. The museum does not serve an active visual arts community, nor can it draw from nearby large population centers." He admonished the Noyeses and said "they could have done more for the arts by swallowing their pride and giving their $4 million to an institution that could have made better use of it."

The *New York Times* ran an equally disparaging review, remarking that other twentieth-century art departments in New Jersey would not have to move over. As for the decoy collection, the best view was from the gallery side where one saw "floor-to-ceiling ducks' butts." The museum never intended to compete with "other twentieth-century art departments." But the ill-informed criticism did little to help the museum's wobbly image.

The reviews were like the city mouse meets the country mouse, with the assumption that the city mouse knows what is best for everyone. Joseph Landau, one of the inaugural exhibition artists, told the *New York Times,* "The southern part of the state has been a cultural desert and really needed this beautiful museum."

A year later, Sozanski was willing to make some concessions to the museum built "in a bird sanctuary...a temple built in a country that had yet to discover religion." He wrote, "The museum apparently is making an impact on previously museum-less southern New Jersey. According to Fabbri, attendance during the first year exceeded her expectations." Quoting Anne, "We are not just drawing from the southern New Jersey area; our shows have begun to attract a sophisticated audience from Philadelphia and New York."

Reviews, good and ambivalent, all helped bring people to the museum. "We were regularly reviewed in the *New York Times,*" Anne said. "Grace Glueck and Bill Zimmer, and of course they loved it. The *Times* would give them a car and driver. We got people coming, especially in the summers, when the New Yorkers would go to Long Beach Island. Then they came down to the museum. What pleased me was that they would always say, wow, this is a real art museum. It's not just a place to see paintings of lighthouses."

Fabbri made substantial headway in obtaining grants for the museum. "I always applied for grants wherever I worked. We got some wonderful grants from the State. In fact, one year Governor Kean gave us, I think, $25,000 that we never even asked for. For excellence in exhibitions. We were so surprised. I don't know what that did to the state budget. He gave us what we applied for, then he gave us extra. I thought it was wonderful he appreciated us." The unexpected gift was a follow-up to Governor Kean's letter of congratulations and support to the museum at the time of its opening.

Anne was confident that the New Jersey State Council on the Arts (NJSCA) would give grants for contemporary or modern art but not for folk art exhibitions. She basically ignored the Noyeses' folk art collection.

Between 1985 and 1991, she applied for and received more than $1.6 million in grants, chiefly from the NJSCA. In 1985, the NJSCA grant was $17,000, and in 1991, it was $70,000, plus $1,092,500 for an auditorium addition. (The grant for the auditorium was never used and reverted back to the state.)

Given the divergent purposes and opinions of the museum, the odd pairing of a scholar as director and a Piney as her assistant worked perfectly. Fabbri's cosmopolitan background and education contrasted dramatically with Gary Giberson's deep roots in the pines. Gary gave decoy-carving demonstrations at 2:00 p.m. every Wednesday through Sunday. His well-honed talents as a demonstrating artist and storyteller became one of the main attractions of the museum. People who knew Gary came just to see him and hear him talk.

By this time, he was a renowned carver. Presidents Johnson, Nixon and Carter had commissioned his work. He was among ten decoy carvers in the country whose pieces were considered worth collecting. A pair of mallards or green winged teals would sell for $600. One day at Wheaton Village, he sold $11,000 worth of carvings and stood in the corner and wept with happiness. He gave Fred and Ethel credit for his fame.

He told visitors, "Fred Noyes, who founded the museum, is my idol and inspiration as an artist and a person." Dressed comfortably in a brown corduroy Piney hat and a leather coverall, Gary straddled a narrow sliver bench and carved cedar harvested from stands on his own land. With a hatchet, drawknife, rasp and carving knife, he could complete a decoy in eight hours from a chunk of white swamp cedar. He finished the wood with a fine sanding and then painted, all the while talking nonstop for several hours, his hands moving from one task to another. The visitor could not help but be infected by Gary's love for his work and for the region. Area schools began to visit the museum, and the children stood spellbound, listening to Gary. Gary brought life to the museum, and people wanted to come back.

Chapter 19

OF FISH AND FOREVER

B esides his work as a renowned carver and demonstrating artist, Gary had another job. He had to bolster Fred's spirits when Fred became unhappy with the foundation and what was going on at the museum.

Niki Giberson explained, "Fred got really frustrated. He kept hitting all these brick walls. Sometimes I didn't think they respected him like they should, the lawyer and the accountant. But the best way to get through to people is not to cuss your head off, and sometimes Fred did that. They would just kind of appease him; he didn't really act businesslike. Ethel always had her composure. There were very few things that he actually cared about enough to get that upset about."

Fred hired the accounting firm of Arthur Andersen and Co. Based on its review, Andersen referred Fred to the Philadelphia law firm of Dechert Price and Rhoads. He hired the firm in June of 1983, the very month the Noyes Museum opened. Herbert Rothenberg and Carl Fiore and their respective firms were subject to investigation for "possible irregularities and overreaching." The Philadelphia firm assigned attorney Stanhope S. Browne to review all work done for Fred and Ethel, including Ethel's estate, three trusts, the foundation, investment recommendations made by Rothenberg and fees and commissions charged.

After researching the background and scope of influence held by Rothenberg and Fiore, Browne concluded, "The relationship between Noyes and Rothenberg was strained from the date of the opening of the museum in June of 1983 when Rothenberg who was presiding at the opening dinner initially failed to acknowledge Noyes' contribution to the creation and funding of the Museum, and did so after all of the other presentations and acknowledgments only after a friend of Noyes' called this omission to the attention of Rothenberg; Noyes was distressed and hurt by this omission.

"While in no way denying the thorough professionalism of Fabbri, and indeed perhaps because of that very professionalism, Noyes believed that she, encouraged by Rothenberg, deprecated his view of what the Museum should be, did not want to display his duck decoys, did not appreciate the art produced by his circle of artist-friends and generally intended to bring the Museum within the more sophisticated realms of the art world and, in Noyes words, the 'piss-ant socialites' who inhabited that world."

A settlement agreement was reached with Rothenberg, Fiore and their counsel and signed on October 23, 1984. The main points of the settlement were to expand the number of foundation trustees from three to six, a commitment from the foundation as to certain exhibits at the museum and a mutual general release of all claims by the foundation against Noyes.

New foundation appointees were respected hotelier and historian Adrian Phillips, Ethel's sister Lois Muller and Fred's friend and professional associate from the New Jersey Travel and Resort Association, John Rogge of Brigantine.

The settlement was a compromise. Fred had wanted the resignations of Rothenberg and Fiore. What irritated him most was that he had to negotiate with the very people he and Ethel had first gone to for professional advice and help regarding the museum and who had been paid substantial fees and commissions for that advice and help.

Fred's continued to be disappointed with the museum. According to Stanhope Browne in his certification, "Noyes struggled with the knowledge that the Museum was not what he and his wife intended, but would nevertheless carry his name into the 21st century and perhaps beyond." Fred did not want his decoy collection to go to the museum because he believed it would not be appreciated there. To best resolve his conflicting feelings, Fred asked Browne to assist with his final will and trust, which was executed on February 19, 1985.

The toll on Fred, now seventy-nine years old, was huge. Fortunately, Fred had other passions.

In 1931, he had written in his application for the Pennsylvania Academy of the Fine Arts, "I study art because I love it, and I expect to paint in the future, but what I will make of it I do not now know." For many years, Fred had to fit his love of art around other obligations. Now painting could be the main event of his day.

Vivid colors leapt off his paint board. The sun and the moon shared places in a brilliant blue sky and were reflected in the water below. Multicolored sails without hulls dodged tilting channel markers, ducks, geese and swans. Swimming fish seemed to smile beneath the variegated layers of the river.

Fred told Niki, who was often nearby when he painted on the porch at the Port Republic house, "You know, if you have the eyes to see it, all of this is going on at one time."

Fish were a consistent subject, suggesting a spiritual dimension, a connection with the universe. *Lazy Fish*, painted in 1983, is a veritable traffic jam of fish swimming horizontally back and forth across vertical highways of green and gold with a black centerline and interspersed with bands of blue. Dead center in the painting is a red fish. This fish is not headed back or forth but straight up. Parallel with the bands of color, the red fish is headed for heaven.

Some of Fred's fish found a home in the chapel he donated to the Mainland Division of the Atlantic City Medical Center in memory of Ethel. In April 1986, the $25,000 chapel was dedicated by Reverend Milton Collins of Port Republic, who seven years earlier had presided over Ethel's funeral. The focal point of the ten- by twenty-foot chapel is a backlit stained-glass panel designed by Fred that hangs over the altar. A large red fish outlined by a yellow, casket-shaped box dominates the design. The fish theme, predominant in the chapel, is also an ancient symbol of Christianity. Other of Fred's art on the walls includes a framed tapestry full of circling fish.

Fred's work was featured at the museum in March 1986. Thirty-nine of his paintings filled one gallery. The event capped some of the most artistically productive years of his life. And finally, he was honored by his museum. "Noyes and His Paintings Are Vivid" was the subtitle of an article in the *Press of Atlantic City* by reporter Laura Italiano. Fred's quick wit shone brightly at the opening, even though at eighty he had slowed physically. He sat quietly, "surrounded by the ingredients of a successful, colorful life. Sixty years' worth of ink, oil and acrylic burst from their canvases in sharp primary colors. They are mostly seascapes, filled with sailboats and waterfowl—the stuff of vivid daydreams from the nationally known artist.

"The octogenarian leans heavily now on the help of a cane and a hearing aid. His friends act as translators for the questions of onlookers, leaning close to shout into his ear. He replies softly, but with a clever wit matching that of his work.

"'Co-founder of the museum? I don't know what that means,' Fred was quoted as saying. 'Oh, unless you mean that $4 million.'"

The article stated Fred painted every day, sometimes two hours, sometimes ten minutes.

"'Oh, I paint to sell. I need the money,' he deadpans, his friends leaning over with laughter in their chairs. 'What paintings should we buy from Fred so he can eat tomorrow,' exclaims one."

Fabbri appreciated Fred's work in that he was not derivative from anyone. She said, "Fred had very much his own style. He created his own language, it was his. I would say it is a very personal vision. I always enjoyed looking at his paintings when I would go to his house. Gary, Carl and I would sit on the porch. Looking at the view, you could see what inspired him.

"Fred was very appreciative of other artists," Fabbri continued. "He'd come to see the shows and discuss the art work with me. He wouldn't say anything at the opening, I was so busy then. But he would come later, on a weekday. His driver would bring him after lunch at Seaview.

"Mel Leipzig was his favorite at the opening show. Fred pointed out the reflections that Mel had in a painting of himself in a van with a rearview mirror and the outside mirror and what they were showing. From there Fred would go off and talk about reflections in general and colors and how colors change when they are reflected in a mirror. I remember his pointing that out and being very interested in that. Nothing much escaped him.

"He said things that showed remarkable observation and visual acuity. But then if I said, 'Oh, yes, that's wonderful, Fred,' he would say, 'Oh well, that's nothing,' and stalk off as if he were embarrassed that he said it. But that was his manner. A defense that he didn't want too much of himself revealed. Yes, I think John Cunningham was right. He preferred very much being the country boy. He would go around and look at the paintings and had these very good comments. But if he thought you were listening too closely, he shut up.

"This was early on. Later he was not feeling up to it."

Fred's spirit remained strong, but his World War II leg wound became more of a problem, and it was increasingly difficult for him to get around. Also, he had diabetes and was becoming deaf. No doubt, ongoing struggles with the trustees took an additional toll on his health.

Along with the Gibersons, Helene Walls was Fred's closest caretaker. This was more than a job for Helene because she loved Fred. She enjoyed his outrageous personality and appreciated his painting. In addition to a salary, he gave her a number of his paintings, a Paul Stankard glass paperweight and a treasured decoy, a rocking head Brandt.

One challenge was to keep him warm. A good friend of Helene's, Joyce Schiereck, remembers, "Fred was very cold in the end, and he would just sit in the den all summer. They had a roaring fire in there, and they had an eating table. I think he had diabetes, poor circulation, so there was a fire summer and winter."

Helene helped entertain Fred's friends when they came to visit. She decorated for Halloween and Thanksgiving and always kept fresh flowers in the house. He loved it. The guests and the decorating gave a familiar sense of comfort, because that was how Ethel had done things.

As the months went by, he resorted to using a wheelchair when he went out. People remember seeing him at a charity benefit or dining in a restaurant in the chair. Fred was in and out of the hospital several times. He was having mini strokes.

Barbara McLaughlin said, "He was very lonely at the end. He used to say he was ready to go. I remember him saying that. He wasn't even painting that much."

Gary Giberson, Fred's unofficial adopted son, was one of the last people to be with Fred. "He had a serious stroke and was in the hospital. I would go in and ask him art questions. I would look at him, and he would be there. I would say, squeeze my hand for yes or no. I would ask if he knew who I was, and he would let me know and he would roll his eyes. I would say, 'Fred, I'm having a hell of a time with this orange. I don't know if I have too much red, or should I use cadmium yellow here?' He was looking at the ceiling, and all of a sudden, he rolled his eyes over and looked at me, and his look said, 'Who the hell are you kidding, you know how to mix orange.' That is the last thing I remember of him. He died the next day."

It was late in the afternoon, and Fred was fading in and out of sleep in his hospital bed. It seemed as he drifted back over the years he found himself sitting in a slowly darkening bar room, the dusky afterglow of sunset before the lights are turned on. He became aware of a sound, a faint crackling sound. The sound became clearer. A voice was calling over the loudspeaker system at Smithville.

"Fred Noyes, Fred Noyes, paging Fred Noyes. Report to the main office. Paging Fred Noyes."

"Okay, Ethel, okay," Fred grumbled, "I'm on my way."

He got off his barstool. "See you later, Bo," he said, winking at the bartender.

Fred left the Lantern Light Tavern to meet Ethel, who was walking briskly along the brick path to meet him.

The *Press of Atlantic City* reported that Fred Winslow Noyes Jr. died at 6:10 p.m. of natural causes at the Atlantic City Medical Center on Tuesday, June 2, 1987. His wife, Ethel Marie Noyes, predeceased him by eight years. There were no immediate survivors.

EPILOGUE

Fred's and Ethel's headstones lie side by side in the Presbyterian Church graveyard on New Jersey Avenue in Absecon, just one block from where they set up their first antique shop. While they rested in peace, the estate entered a period of turmoil. Legal documents and false accusations abounded.

Fred's will caused fireworks. He had drawn up four wills during the emotionally stressful time from December 1982 to October 1983. After the settlement with Rothenberg and Fiore in 1984, Fred executed his final will and estate plan in February 1985 with his attorney, Stanhope Browne. The First National Bank of Tom's River was appointed executor and trustee. The will established a perpetual trust for the benefit of the museum. Thus the museum had an annual source of interest income, but the principal was not to be invaded.

Lawsuits followed. The foundation wanted direct control of the estate. Fiore said, "We need the money now. We don't need it over the next fifty years." "It's a technical issue, really," said Herbert Rothenberg, "We say the trust is superfluous." Reporter G. Patrick Pawling wrote, "It might seem that the foundation would be satisfied with a nest egg of several million dollars. But it wants to control those dollars. It wants it all in one big gulp."

Additionally, Fred's will stated: "I direct my executor to sell all my remaining decoys and carvings not done by Gary Giberson, my paintings and other collections...and to add the proceeds to my residuary estate." All the items went to the Bourne Auction House in Hyannis, Massachusetts. Fred took control from the grave. He had his precious decoys sold to strangers rather than fall into the hands of Rothenberg and Fiore. Gary Giberson was sent to the auction to bid on and buy specific items for the museum. It was not a happy assignment for Gary.

Gary said, "Everything was done through Bourne on March 11 and 12, 1988. The auction grossed $315,285. Fred had so many decoys they couldn't sell them all at one time. There was a second auction on June 28 and 29."

Gary was allotted a specific amount of money to bid on certain pieces for the museum. The auction was well attended. Often when Gary hit his limit, the bird sold on the next bid to someone else. But his bidding drove up the price of the decoys, and consequently, more money was made for the museum.

Hundreds of paintings Fred had done over the years also came under dispute. According to Andrew Newman, "Fred's art was well received. Unfortunately, after he passed away, the estate was pretty much locked up for a long time because of the lawyers. We stored the collection of Fred's work and became the caretakers for about fifteen years. The Noyes Museum never showed any interest in his work until recently."

Fortunately, that has changed. The return of the collection to the museum resulted in an exhibit from October 7, 2000, to February 4, 2001. "Fred Returns" featured "Selected Works by Fred W. Noyes from the Permanent Collection." In 2005, there was a centennial exhibit in celebration of Fred's 100th birthday.

The Noyeses' home, the historic Franklin Inn on the Mill Pond in Port Republic, was listed for sale at $750,000. It was bought and lovingly restored by Joyce Schiereck, herself an artist, collector and friend of Helene Walls. The house and grounds are meticulously maintained. The historic landmark is a source of pride for the quiet town.

Memories of Fred and Ethel remain etched in the stories of family and friends. As time passes, however, there are fewer living people who knew this amazing couple. Fifty years ago, everyone in the area knew of Fred and Ethel Noyes. Today, few people know that the Historic Towne of Smithville, the Ram's Head Inn and the Noyes Museum all exist because of them.

Smithville had a number of owners after it was bought by American Broadcasting Company. Some plundered the artifacts collected by the Noyeses, and others took their profits but let the historic Inn and buildings fall into disrepair. Quail Hill, the museum-like restaurant complex, was torn down in August 1996. The Freehold Barn was spared because the township wanted to preserve the architecture. A year later, on September 20, 1997, the *Press* reported, "A suspicious fire ripped through the old Freehold Barn late on a Friday night, destroying the last remaining vestige of Quail Hill Inn." The land remains vacant.

Fortunately, on January 31, 1997, the inn and original shops on the east side of the footbridge were purchased by Tony and Fran Coppola and Charles and Laura Bushar. The Coppolas and the Bushars have done an outstanding job of bringing new life to Smithville. Like the Noyeses before them, the Coppolas take on broad responsibilities. Fran, for example, runs the Candle Shoppe and designed the signature Inn Salad, complete with cranberries. Tony served as president of the board of directors of the Noyes Museum and continues to be an active board member.

Twenty-five years after the Noyeses left Smithville, 115 former employees gathered for a reunion in April 1999. Fran Coppola took the podium in the Great Bay Room and told how she still talks to Ethel Noyes for guidance and advice. If a big event such as the Mayfest is coming up, and bad weather looms in the forecast, Fran looks up to the heavens and says, "Ethel, what would you do now? How would you handle this?" In closing, Fran stated, "We can't make Smithville like it was when the Noyeses ran it, but we are doing our best. We respect what they created and how they ran their business."

The Historic Village on the west side of the footbridge was acquired by Ed and Wendie Fitzgerald. The old structures now house a variety of shops, a small restaurant and a bed-and-breakfast. To attract families, there is a carousel, a little train to ride and paddle boats. The Fitzgeralds are conservators of the history of the area.

The Ram's Head Inn remains one of the fine dining restaurants of the area, a sought-after location for weddings and other private parties.

There have been six directors at the Noyes Museum since Anne Fabbri left in 1991. The current director, Michael Cagno, was hired in 2006 and brings knowledge of local arts to the job. His plans include collaboration with other institutions throughout the state to bring more artists and larger audiences to the museum. In January 2011, the museum successfully completed negotiations with the nearby Richard Stockton College of New Jersey. The two institutions have a ten-year agreement whereby the college assists the museum financially and the museum provides opportunities and internships for students in the arts and other departments.

This author was invited to give a presentation at the museum during Women's History Month on March 8, 2001. It would have been Ethel's ninetieth birthday. Before I said a word to the audience, I showed a dozen slides of buildings, including the Franklin Inn, the Smithville Inn and shops, the Ram's Head Inn and the Noyes Museum. The images presented in silence were powerful. These buildings are the permanent legacy Fred and Ethel made to this area.

There is a legacy other than buildings and works of art. That is the history and the stories recorded in this book.

BIBLIOGRAPHY

I n addition to interviews, I researched the Noyeses and relevant local history in newspapers, primarily the *Press of Atlantic City*, books, periodicals, legal documents and other sources. These are documented below:

Ascher, Sid. "Makes Old Houses New." *Press of Atlantic City*, July 26, 1974.

———. "Old Village Museum." *Press of Atlantic City*, January 27, 1974.

———. "Smithville 'Backs Up' to Success." *Press of Atlantic City*, January 27, 1974.

———. "Smithville Is a Planning Museum Village Project." *Press of Atlantic City*, January 28, 1973.

Baker, Penny. "Noyes Museum Enriches New Jersey's Cultural Landscape." *Press of Atlantic City*, May 22, 1983.

Beck, Henry. *Jersey Genesis*. New Brunswick, NJ: Rutgers University Press, 1945, 1963.

Bolton, Elizabeth, Martha Hester and Cynthia Mason. *The Atlantic County Cookbook*. Published by the Atlantic County Cultural and Heritage Advisory Board and the Atlantic County Office of Cultural Affairs. Egg Harbor City, NJ: Laureate Press, 1976.

Boucher, Jack E. *Absegami: Yesteryear.* Published by the Atlantic County Historical Society. Egg Harbor City, NJ: Laureate Press, 1963.

Browne, Stanhope S. *Certification.* October 13, 1987.

Corrado, Frank. "Past and Present Merge at Smithville: More than Textbook History." *Press of Atlantic City*, May 23, 1973.

Cunningham, John T. "The Wonderful World of Smithville Inn." *New Jersey Business Magazine*, November 1966.

Davis, Ed. *Atlantic City Diary: A Century of Memories, 1880–1985.* McKee City, NJ: Atlantic Sunrise, 1980.

Deming, Ruth Z. "A Museum Is Built." *Art Matters* 2, no. 9 (June 1983).

Dietz, Ulysses Grant. *Paul Stankard, Homage to Nature.* Photographs by John Bigelow Taylor. New York: Harry N. Abrams, 1996.

Ewing, Sarah W.R., and Robert McMullin. *Along Absecon Creek: A History of Early Absecon, New Jersey.* Originally published 1965. Commemorative edition, 1991, printed by C.O.W.A.N. Printing, Bridgeton, NJ. Bound by National Publishing Company, Philadelphia, PA.

Foundation Directory, U.S. Documents Librarian, Foundation Collection. Supervisor Teri Taylor, References Services, NJ State Library.

Guyette, Schmidt and Deeter. The World's Leading Decoy Auctions Firm, est. 1984. www.guyetteandschmidt.com.

Historic Smithville Inns, Incorporated. Annual Report, 1973.

Hitzel, Ed. "The Stump Jumper Who Made a Million." *Press of Atlantic City*, April 12, 1981.

McMahon, William. *Historic Towne of Smithville.* Egg Harbor City, NJ: Laureate Press, 1967 and 1975.

————. *Tales of Historic Smithville Inn.* Egg Harbor City, NJ: Laureate Press, 1965.

McPhee, John. *The Pine Barrens.* New York: Farrar, Straus and Giroux, 1967.

Press of Atlantic City. Numerous news articles from 1966 to 1989.

Raynor, Vivian. "A New Museum Joins the Ranks." *New York Times*, July 31, 1983.

Rothenberg, Herbert. Errors, Omissions and Distortions Set Forth in the Certification of Stanhope S. Browne, October 13, 1987.

Sander, Harriet S. *Sketches of Old Port Republic.* New Jersey Tercentenary Year, 1964. Port Republic Tercentenary Committee.

Schwartz, Sonny. "South Jersey Love Affair." *Press of Atlantic City*, November 19, 1972.

Smith, David. "Record Price: $830,000 for Elmer Crowell's Decoy 'Feeding Plover.'" *Antiques and the Arts Online*, December 5, 2006.

Smithville Banner, vol. 15, 1970; vol. 19, 1972, published by Historic Towne of Smithville, NJ.

Trakel, David. "Outbreak, the 1918 Flu Epidemic." *Philadelphia Inquirer*, October 4, 1998.

Young, Eugene V., and Elaine Conover Abrahamson. *The Story of Galloway Township.* Published by The Galloway Township Bicentennial Committee. Egg Harbor City, NJ: Laureate Press, 1976.

Index

ABOUT THE AUTHOR

Judy Courter and her family moved to Port Republic, New Jersey, in 1972, near the home of Fred and Ethel Noyes. Intrigued by the rich past of this former shipbuilding settlement, Judy was one of the founding members of the town's historical society. She and her husband, Joe, and their three young children often visited nearby Smithville.

Years later, Judy was struck by the fact that nothing was written about the Noyeses, an amazing couple who made a lasting contribution to South Jersey's history, economy and culture. When she began to research, interview and give presentations, she discovered everyone had a story about Fred and Ethel.

Donna Andrews Photography.

Judy graduated from Mount Holyoke College in Massachusetts with a degree in American history. She is on the board of the Noyes Museum of Art of Stockton College, a lifetime member of the Atlantic County Historical Society and a member of the Absecon Historical Society.

Judy and Joe now live in Absecon and enjoy their large collection of Fred Noyes paintings.